FUNDRAI$ING FOR HONOR$
A HANDBOOK

by

Larry R. Andrews

Jeffrey A. Portnoy

Georgia Perimeter College

jeffrey.portnoy@gpc.edu

General Editor, NCHC Monograph Series

Published in 2009 by

National Collegiate Honors Council

110 Neihardt Residence Center

University of Nebraska-Lincoln

540 N. 16th Street

Lincoln, NE 68588-0627

(402) 472-9150

FAX: (402) 472-9152

Email: nchc@unlserve.unl.edu

http://www.NCHChonors.org

International Standard Book Number 978-0-9796659-9-8

Managing Editor: Mitch Pruitt
Production Editor: Cliff Jefferson
Wake Up Graphics, Birmingham, AL

Printed by EBSCO Media, Birmingham, AL

TABLE OF CONTENTS

Introduction 5

Chapter 1:
Baby Steps: Getting Started 9
  Barriers to Honors Fundraising Success 10
  Institutional Context 11
  Filthy Lucre: How Can Honors Use It? 13
  Building an Alumni Donor Base 14
    Communications 17
    Events. 21
    Organization 23
    Solicitation 24
  Stewardship 101: Effective Written Communications 27
    Procedures. 28
    Content 29
  Securing the Support of Top Administrators. 35
  Getting to Know the Development Office 37
  Developing Modest Projects. 41
  Exploring Grant Funding. 45

Chapter 2:
Finding the Pace: Increasing the Momentum 53
  Stewardship 301: Donor Activities 53
    Events. 53
    Recognition 55
  Creating a Fundraising Plan 56
  Acquiring Some Formal Training 65
  Developing More Ambitious Projects. 67
  Writing Effective Case Statements 71
  Making Fundraising Processes Systematic 77
  Making Cold Calls and Listening to Donors 82
    Preparation 83
    The Meeting. 86
  Writing Grants 89
  Making Public Relations Systematic. 98
  Securing and Building Unrestricted Funds 100

Chapter 3:

Bold Strides: Becoming a Pro! 103

Making Honors Prominent in a Capital Campaign 103

Establishing and Working with an Advisory Board 106

Creating Naming Opportunities 108

Developing Transformative Projects 110

Scholarships 110

Facilities 114

Artist/Lecture Series 115

Professorships 117

Endowing the Program or College! 122

Conclusion 125

Appendix A:

Glossary 127

Appendix B:

NCHC E-mail Survey, Fall 2007 131

Appendix C:

Sample Documents 135

1. Thank-You Letters 135

2. Thesis Sponsorship Solicitation and Reply Form 137

3. Mail Reply Forms, with Options to Donate 140

4. Student Publicity Waivers 142

5. Press Release for a Hometown Newspaper 144

6. Case Statements 145

7. Contact Notes 150

Appendix D:

Annotated Bibliography 153

LARRY R. ANDREWS

INTRODUCTION

To many honors administrators, fundraising is alien and frightening. After all, we come from the faculty, and, dedicated as we are to the noble ideals of learning, we do not care for filthy lucre (except in the form of grant support for our research!). What we cannot imagine is personally *asking strangers for money*.

This monograph begins with several assumptions. First, honors deans and directors are relatively inexperienced at fundraising and may feel daunted by it. Many of us lack the time and travel budget to visit donor prospects, busy as we are with commitments to our programs and perhaps teaching and doing research as well. Even when fundraising is part of our job description, we may push it to the bottom of our list of priorities. Many of us do not have assigned development officers to nudge us along and to help us find likely donor prospects. Our institutions may lack a strong tradition in fundraising as well. Without such support, our fundamental distaste for fundraising remains unchecked.

A second assumption, however, is that honors administrators are increasingly expected to play an active role in fundraising. Some private institutions and a few major state universities have accumulated generous alumni and friends and remarkable endowments. Yet they and most public institutions are increasingly strapped for operating funds as state support declines, tuition rises, endowment investments fluctuate, and student financial aid, limited by declining government grants, carries the curse of increasing debt burdens. Development work has become increasingly professionalized, but high turnover in that profession and the growing number of major capital campaigns mean that academic leaders must be more and more involved in telling the story of their success and their vision for the future. Honors programs may be neglected in the push for funding for showcase disciplinary programs and for facilities, so the honors administrator may be expected to take more solo initiative for fundraising than other academic leaders such as deans and chairs. Finally, judging from National Collegiate Honors Council (NCHC) conference sessions, interest in fundraising among honors leaders is rapidly increasing. The motivation is there.

A third assumption is that fundraising for honors can yield results and can even be exciting. External financial support is not designed to replace the institution's responsibility for funding our programs, but it can provide flexibility for various projects and initiatives otherwise unthinkable in the internal budget climate. Honors has a good story to tell in attracting donors. It represents academic quality. It gives students high challenge and warm support in the form of small classes and personal attention. It offers, in its students' success, many heartwarming arguments for support, especially for scholarships and for special programs, such as study abroad or research support. There really are people who would delight in being associated with such quality. And once they feel good about their donations, our good stewardship will maintain them as allies and friends who may increase their donations in the future.

This monograph is directed primarily to honors deans and directors, who have widely varying experience with fundraising. It may also be useful reading for those staff members, faculty, and development officers who have some responsibility for honors fundraising. It focuses on what the honors academic leader can bring to fundraising efforts. It is not written for, or from the perspective of, professional development officers. (For any technical terms I do use, consult the Glossary in Appendix A.) Nor does it suggest ways for honors leaders to increase their budget allocation from the institution. Nor is it concerned with fundraising activities by honors student organizations undertaken in support of the groups' own events or of charitable causes (e.g., Relay for Life), except where the role of students or, say, the sale of paraphernalia supports the broader fundraising plan of the honors college or program.[*]

Because many honors administrators face fundraising with inexperience, dread, and even hostility, I have organized the work developmentally, beginning with the easiest stages of initiation and progressing toward greater challenges. Honors leaders more experienced in fundraising may choose to skim over the early parts to arrive at sections more relevant to their level of experience. Readers, of course, may consult only those topics with which they are least familiar. Other sources, some listed in the bibliography, can provide a more analytic breakdown of the different aspects of fundraising planning, procedure, and management. Some offer detailed instruction and advice on such topics as writing a good case statement. The structure I have used reflects my own learning process as I moved from a faculty member utterly innocent of fundraising to an experienced dean reasonably comfortable with all aspects of the process.

Any fundraising success I enjoyed as a 14-year dean of a large and well-established university honors college depended on the warm

---

[*] Because, for simplicity, I will often refer only to honors programs, please understand that term to include honors colleges as well. Similarly, references to honors directors also include deans.

generosity of many donors—often alumni—who believed in the honors mission and the quality of our students and program. In compiling this monograph, I am indebted to my wife Karen, to my students and staff, to the numerous development officers and donors with whom I have worked, and to my honors colleagues nationally who have furnished a rich array of ideas and practices in surveys, interviews, publications, and NCHC conference sessions. Some of their stories are included here anonymously, to preserve confidentiality; one of the first lessons of fundraising is discretion.

CHAPTER 1:
BABY STEPS:
GETTING STARTED

When I applied for the position of Dean of the Honors College at my university in 1993, I noted with a tremor the expectations of fundraising (anathema!) spelled out in the job description. Perhaps I thought that if I performed all of the other duties well—including overseeing the university's general education program—no one would notice that I was postponing thinking about fundraising until the indefinite and preferably distant future. I was an experienced honors faculty member, knew the students and staff, and was assured by colleagues that I could handle, despite being untested at the time, the management tasks of an administrative post. Going out to raise money, however, was a totally alien concept. When I finally did begin to have modest success at raising money, it first came as an unintended consequence of other activities. Hence one of the first lessons of this book: *Starting small is OKAY.*

My discomfort with fundraising is echoed by the results of an informal survey I conducted in fall 2007 among honors administrators, using the NCHC listserve. (For the original questionnaire, see Appendix B.) Of the several hundred subscribers, 60 responded to the survey. A number of respondents were experienced and comfortable with fundraising, and perhaps they were the ones most likely to respond. Many, however, expressed little experience with fundraising and even less comfort at the thought. Of the respondents, 65% reported fundraising as 5% or less of their honors work, with 28% at zero. (Only 62% were full-time administrators.) At the same time, 40% said that fundraising was part of their job description, and 42% said that fundraising was increasingly an expectation from the upper administration. About 65% of the respondents reported some help in fundraising from the development office, but 17% reported no help of any kind.

Regarding comfort level, the majority of respondents reported feeling comfortable with sending thank-you letters for donations, "talking up" their programs, and working with their institution's central development office. When it came to holding fundraising receptions, meeting potential donors alone, and involving students in meeting donors or potential donors, the comfort level diminished. Respondents were least comfortable with telephoning potential donors, involving honors faculty in fundraising, soliciting donations from parents, and asking a potential donor for a gift of a specific amount.

In the spirit of camaraderie and support that characterizes the NCHC conferences and listserve, the survey respondents offered positive encouragement to the beginner: "Do it, regardless of how uncomfortable it makes you," "Just get started," "At least bring it up . . . give it a shot," "Patience," "Get help," "Keep plugging away." I sorely needed these assurances in 1993!

Barriers to Honors Fundraising Success

If those assurances sound facile, if stories of unexpected endowment gifts stretch credulity, if fear and distaste have become habitual and convenient, the time has come for honors directors to confront some of the other obstacles that may stand in the way before moving toward concrete methods of becoming engaged. If testing the fundraising waters remains daunting, there may be some good reasons, not just fear and inexperience. It is not entirely a matter of attitude.

When I asked survey respondents to state the greatest barrier to honors fundraising success, the conditions they cited ranged widely from the individuals themselves, or the nature of their position, to the institution. Some respondents referred to qualities in themselves such as timidity, inexperience, or discomfort. Others noted a failure to tailor their request to the interests of a potential donor, their own lack of initiative in establishing a relationship with the development office, or sheer unwillingness to deal with that aspect of university functioning when there are professionals with that responsibility. More respondents, however, referred to limitations inherent in their job duties: lack of time because of their ongoing projects, lack of staff to help organize the effort, or the absence or the low priority of fundraising in their job description. A few cited lack of sufficient alumni, predominance of young alumni without giving capacity, or alumni defined more by their college or department affiliation than by their membership in honors.

Most survey respondents, however, located the barriers to honors fundraising in their institutions. Almost a quarter of them said that their institution discouraged their involvement in fundraising for honors. Several noted that their development office requires all funds raised to go into a general budget, selects only a few university-wide projects for fundraising, or makes everyone responsible for honors fundraising with the result that no one takes responsibility. A further problem is simply securing the attention of the administration and the development office, either of which may (a) dictate the direction of fundraising without consultation with honors; (b) show stubbornness in understanding how honors works, including the perception that higher-ability students do not need financial aid; or (c) assign constituent development officers to disciplinary colleges but let honors slip through the cracks. Some respondents cited lack of fundraising coordination in general and excessive bureaucratization of fundraising. A number of respondents found that institutional structure itself was an obstacle: "All Honors College alums are also alums of some other unit in the University." Thus several mentioned that competition with other areas on campus and especially with college deans made fundraising for honors challenging.

This litany of the obstacles honors leaders face in raising money for their programs, along with their central and time-consuming concerns in directing effective academic programs, explains why they often accomplish little in the way of fundraising. Before shifting the mood in this handbook toward positive advice, we must pause for an oft-expressed caveat: The institutional issues just cited remind us that institutional context and culture, and honors programs themselves, are stunningly diverse.

Institutional Context

Honors programs and their institutions vary widely. Although honors programs share an educational mission dedicated to students of high ability and motivation, they range from 20 to over 5,000 students in population, from program to college in status, from 1 year to 80 years of existence. They serve a variety of student populations and have varying admission criteria. Some survive on a shoestring budget and a volunteer faculty director, while others enjoy a multi-million-dollar endowment in a state-of-the-art facility under a full-time dean and its own faculty. Some programs report to a dean and others to a provost or other administrator. Some have no courses of their own, others a highly structured curriculum and even degree-granting authority. Some focus exclusively on honors students, while others administer university-wide programs such as fellowship or event coordination. Such diversity has made many members of NCHC reluctant to mandate standards or benchmark characteristics.

Similarly, at the risk of stating the obvious, institutions housing honors programs range from two-year colleges to research universities. They may be public or private, secular or religious, small or huge. They may do little for fundraising or engage only the president in this activity, or they may have a large central or decentralized development office headed by a vice president. They may never have engaged in a capital campaign, or they may be on their sixth such campaign and have a well-researched database of donor prospects. They may or may not place heavy expectations on their academic leaders to raise money. Their structures and processes for fundraising vary widely and change over time. Relations between development and honors range from intimate to hostile, depending on the institution. Private institutions have generally practiced fundraising for a longer time, with more investment of resources and with more success; they depend on philanthropy for a significant percentage of their operating budgets. Many public institutions started serious development work only as state support dwindled.

Frequent turnover characterizes both development personnel and honors administrators, further challenging continuity and consistency in fundraising efforts. The perspectives of professional fundraisers and honors academics may be at odds, and their respective roles in fundraising not always clearly enunciated. Honors leaders themselves, as noted in my survey results, have widely varying experience in fundraising, including, for many, no experience whatsoever. For some the concept of donor support is either an alien idea or a seemingly unattainable dream. Yet in some cases honors is allocated a dedicated development officer, secretarial support, and expense reimbursement, and the honors director or dean may be spending a third or more of her or his time seeking donor financial support alongside the development officer. Such collaborations include strategic planning, writing case statements for support, calling and meeting with prospects, organizing events, keeping current donors happy and well-informed, and issuing publicity statements—all resulting in a steady stream of donations and some occasional endowment gifts.

Because of this teeming diversity of honors programs, their institutions, and their leaders' experience, a fundraising handbook must offer a variety of methods and examples. Although all of my own academic experience has occurred at public research universities, I hope that what I offer here will also resonate with honors leaders at two-year colleges and liberal arts colleges, with or without religious affiliations, and with both neophytes and veterans. Colleagues from a variety of institutions have generously shared their knowledge and examples of the fundraising adventure and misadventure. Some methods may not work at all in some institutional contexts. On the other hand, some ideas or stories here may inspire readers to instigate change in their institution's standard practices. Regardless of each honors program's context, history, and size, raising donor support is not only desirable but possible.

Moreover, fundraising for honors and for higher education in general possesses a new urgency, and not just because of difficult economic times. For several decades the funding support for higher education, particularly for state institutions, has been eroding. State-supported institutions have become state-assisted institutions, and some barely that. How can an institution cope with a dramatic shrinkage of state support over 20 years, in one example, from 85% of the cost of education to 23%? Students and their families compensate by paying ever higher tuition. Institutions pursue private dollars with increasing fervor. The result is that fundraising has become everyone's direct or indirect concern, and honors directors now share this pressure with other academic leaders. This increasingly shared responsibility unites all of us in higher education and in honors circles, despite the diversity of our programs and institutions. Honors leaders inexperienced at securing private donations need to begin thinking seriously about what fundraising specifically for honors could do for their programs and how they can go about it.

Filthy Lucre: How Can Honors Use It?

No, I am not joking. Amazingly enough, some honors programs are well funded by their institutions. Many small programs are poorly funded, but their often part-time directors have neither the responsibility nor the time for fundraising. In both cases, honors administrators may not be able to imagine how donor money could be spent. Scholarships may be covered centrally. No staff members are available to initiate a special project to enhance student learning. Salaries are already accounted for in the budget. Students seem content with what they have and are not complaining.

Although directors may be so consumed with running the existing program that they have little time for imagining new projects, a good case for doing more can always be made, and someone out there may be interested in financing it. To quote Bob Spurrier, one of our wise national honors leaders, "Always have a wish list!" Does the honors program have an annual event honoring graduating seniors? What if it could be a more splendid ceremony if the expense were underwritten by a local business? Do only a limited number of students attend research conferences or honors conferences? What if an alum paid the registration or lodging costs for them so that more could attend? Do students have expenses associated with completing a thesis? What if a local civic organization reimbursed those costs in exchange for having the student present the research at a meeting? Are students rejecting study abroad because it means additional debt? What if an alum who participated in such a program offered enough scholarship support to get that student to Leipzig or Capetown or Tokyo?

Even such small gifts can change lives. But large donations can transform the landscape on a grand scale. Could honors have a scholarship program of its own, in addition to what students receive through university aid? An endowed fund would provide freshman renewable scholarships in perpetuity and could be named for the donor. An endowed artist-lecture series could enrich the intellectual experience of students and faculty. With an adequate gift, the honors program could offer incoming students a first-class orientation retreat as an introduction to the intellectual community. An endowed professorship could provide an additional stipend to a highly regarded but hard-to-obtain faculty member for a special-topics honors course. Facilities always seem inadequate. The right donor might offer funding to remodel or even to construct a new honors center, or at least to go halves with the institution for its funding.

Those less experienced at fundraising do not have to think only in terms of major gifts. Certainly such gifts can make the biggest difference: development professionals realize that at least 90% of the funds donated come from 10% of the donors. Later in this handbook we can focus more on those large gifts, as well as engage the debate over how fundraising effort should best be spent, but for now we will concentrate on some small, easy, and even obvious ways to generate donor funds. Despite the power of major gifts, directors should never marginalize small donors. Small gifts can become larger gifts over time, and the honors program will benefit from the long-term relationship with a satisfied but initially small donor. Where is an obvious place to start small? Directors themselves should become donors to their programs. How can they ask others to give if they have not given? And how better for directors to feel the donor's point of view and motivation? But the next obvious place for directors to start is with their own students, of course, as alumni.

Building an Alumni Donor Base

Staying in touch with honors alumni keeps them engaged with the program and establishes an excellent base of potential donors who have benefited from being in honors and who may feel affection for and loyalty to the program.[*] This perception was one of the lessons of unintended consequences I learned early on as a dean. By reviving an alumni newsletter and establishing an alumni council, I soon discovered that the

---

[*] Although in my own program I prefer to use all four forms of this word—for number and gender ("alumnus," "alumna," "alumni," "alumnae"), and although female students are usually the majority, I will bow to popular usage and use the less cumbersome "alumni" for both genders and singular and plural, sometimes skirting the problem by using "alums."

14

number of honors donors greatly increased. Their donations were usually small gifts of $25 or $50, but most donors repeated their gifts, and some later contributed much larger amounts. Strong alumni relations are rewarding in themselves, and fundraising does not always have to be the ulterior motive in conducting them. But they will lead naturally to future financial support.

Having a well-established program with alumni now in mid or late career with prime capacity for giving is a stroke of luck. My own program began in 1933 and became a college in 1965, and I have had regular contact with our alumni, including some donors from the 1930s. Even if a program is too small or too recently established to have much of an alumni body, alumni of any age may have a stronger emotional connection to honors than in a large program because of the close sense of community they experienced. This connectedness is an advantage to exploit. If a program is only 10 years old, and many of its alumni are still in graduate school, are establishing families, or are paying off college loans, the strategy should be to keep them informed about the program, ask them for career updates, and even ask them for small donations to help the next generation of honors students and to begin a habit of philanthropy. If the honors program is housed in a two-year institution and the alumni are now working or have moved on to four-year institutions and graduated, they are still alumni. They may have spent well more than two years getting their associate's degree and feel more connected to the honors program that nurtured them in their formative college years than to the honors program from which they graduated with a bachelor's degree. Some of my honors students came from the two-year honors programs at our regional campuses, and I was well aware that many of them had formed lasting attachments there that we did not supersede. For fundraising purposes, the concept of alumni may include not just those who completed all honors requirements and graduated with an honors designation but also those who perhaps withdrew or transferred after three years in the program.

A good system of record-keeping is a necessity for efficient alumni relations and for fundraising among alumni. For example, programs that maintain an advising folder for each student should continue to maintain it after the student transfers or graduates. When I became dean, I found in a storeroom a box of such folders for each graduation year going back four decades. Because year of graduation was far less useful than name as a key for information retrieval, I organized in cheap used filing cabinets one alphabetical file of folders for all alumni. To each file we readily added any alumni updates and survey responses, news items, and continuing correspondence, including thank-yous for donations. These folders have become a treasure of information as my development officer and I have prepared to meet potential donors. Directors can store old files electronically by scanning new documents and adding them to the alumni e-folders. In any case, directors should abide by their institution's guidelines about secure storage of student information.

An early step in establishing organized alumni relations within honors is discovering who else is keeping track of honors alumni. How active and efficient is the institution's alumni office? Does it produce an alumni magazine and have a web presence? Does it sponsor programs that connect current students to alumni and bring alumni back to campus? Does it have a reliable database with up-to-date contact information? Are honors alums coded or marked as such in the database? Whose responsibility is it to code them as honors graduates? How aware of honors is the alumni office? Have honors alums been members or chairs of the alumni association national board of directors, as ours have? Are other colleges or departments at the institution also tracking their alumni, some of whom would have participated in honors?

Ascertaining the answers to these questions will likely require initiative. Even if the registrar codes student records to show honors status, certification of honors completion by the honors program may be necessary. Such coding must also distinguish honors graduates from those with Latin honors. Directors may have to argue that an honors alumni organization deserves support alongside the overlapping disciplinary alumni councils or regional alumni chapters. Directors may want to offer story ideas or specific alumni accomplishments for the alumni magazine to feature. Directors may find that they are catching up to other units on campus, but at least they will benefit from established procedures already in place. On the other hand, if not much is happening in alumni relations, honors directors can be leaders on this frontier, which is part of the role for honors at any institution. Directors might add to their budget wish list some funds to produce an annual newsletter. Asserting the identity of honors and of honors culture in our institutions, including in alumni relations, is critically important. Many honors alumni, after all, feel a stronger connection to their honors home than to their department or college home.

Although many academics think of alumni only as graduates, many institutions, especially the prestigious private universities and liberal arts colleges, start talking to their current students, and not just their graduating seniors, about their future role as alumni. Certainly many of us express at our ceremonies for seniors the hope that they will stay in touch and give back, but institutions with a strong sense of identity cultivate an alumni attitude in their incoming students. Letters of acceptance, orientation programs, and opening ceremonies provide occasions for encouraging new students to envision successful completion of their degree and a role of lifetime connection to the alma mater. So even at the beginning of thinking about alumni relations, the target audience should be broad.

The initial actions to develop alumni relations and the ensuing fundraising activity are fairly easy. Directors should communicate well with alumni, plan events that engage them, develop an organization at some point, and solicit their donations.

Communications

Once honors programs have established a mailing list for their alumni, they rely on a newsletter, typically an annual one, to stay in touch. This newsletter can be effective not only in touting the accomplishments of students and of the program itself, but also in securing updated contact information. My alumni responded warmly to our newsletter, especially after a newsletter hiatus of some years, because they felt that we cared about keeping in touch and learning about their career progress. As mentioned earlier, we immediately experienced a surge in the number of small donations even without having asked. The two most important ingredients in a newsletter are, of course, news about the program, but also a tear-off reply form that provides information about the alum.

An annual newsletter can

- review major events of the past year,
- give statistics, such as the size of the incoming class or the average grade point average of graduating seniors,
- offer a greeting or column from the director or dean,
- profile a new faculty or staff member,
- spotlight an interesting alum,
- and tell stories of special student achievements such as unusual leadership, conference presentations, service projects, prizes, or prestigious graduate fellowships such as the Truman or the Goldwater.

In this communication, as in all others that have an impact on fundraising, a shrewd strategy is to talk about the quality of the program rather than to dwell on its need for support. A general principle of educational fundraising that will recur throughout this handbook is that *donors respond more readily to quality than to need*, to positive accomplishment than to negative wishfulness. Sometimes a special newsletter can focus on a new initiative, a new facility, or a special event such as a key anniversary.

Both special-purpose and general newsletters should always include the tear-off reply form. Every communication should provide an opportunity to update alumni records and find alumni who will take an interest in the current program. The form should include home and work addresses and telephone numbers (including cell), preferred email address, job title, additional education after leaving the honors program, and check-off boxes or blanks indicating potential interest in (a) returning to campus to talk to current honors students, whether about practical career advice or about specialized knowledge (e.g., a lecture on the bioethics of stem-cell research), (b) offering "shadowing" opportunities or internships, or (c) joining or working with the honors alumni organization. (See a sample form in Appendix C.) Enclosing the pre-paid addressed return envelope typical of most mail solicitations for donations is unnecessary because alumni will usually not mind putting the form in an envelope and paying for the postage. Honors alumni usually do well in life and are proud to share their career progress. When these forms arrive, directors should respond promptly to any show of interest, or the alumni will believe that the attempts to establish connections lack sincerity.

Aside from news, the newsletter should (a) remind alumni of how to contact the honors program and view its website, (b) emphasize the value of the reply form, and (c) briefly instruct alumni on how to make a donation to a general fund or scholarship fund—whatever unrestricted account is most useful on an ongoing basis. Obviously the newsletter must be attractive, readable, impeccably proofread, and fun. A student or the institution's communications office should design an appropriate masthead. If affordable, photographs or student art will enhance the publication. Engaging students to write stories is good training for them and is welcomed by alumni, who probably valued the program in the first place partly for such opportunities to be involved. Depending on the complexity of the newsletter, the lead time must be ample. Directors should determine if a fall kick-off issue will work best, or whether an academic-year-end issue seems more suitable. The goal is to reach readers when they may have more leisure to read it and then to be consistent in mailing it at that same time each year.

Funding for such an annual newsletter need not be an insuperable obstacle, depending on the honors budget, current postage rates, the size of the audience, and the size and quality of the newsletter itself. The very least financial investment could allow for simply photocopying a black-and-white, two-sided sheet, either 8-½ x 11 or 11 x 14, stuffing envelopes, and sending them bulk mail, which will require more lead time. Even if such a minimal effort could occur only once every two years, the point is to get started. A more substantial newsletter might involve a commercial printer, blue ink, and folding and addressing without need of an envelope. At the high end of the spectrum, some programs produce glossy 20–30-page newsmagazines in color with plentiful photographs of students, faculty, and alumni. Honors deans and directors often send these, as well as more modest versions, not only to alumni but also to donors and university or college administrators. Directors should know the cultural values of the program and the institution: Will a modest newsletter look frugal and sensible, or will it look cheap, as if the institution does not care about the program and the program does not care about its alumni? Will a glitzy newsletter convey the program's quality and professionalism, or will it give the impression that the program either has too much money already or spends it on the wrong things?

An additional or alternative alumni communication medium is an electronic newsletter, or e-letter. The major advantage of e-letters is cost—they are free except for the time for composing. The major challenge of e-letters is maintaining a reliable and up-to-date list of e-mail addresses. Many alumni will also not want yet another e-mail message cluttering their mailboxes, especially if unsolicited. Some may recycle a paper newsletter without looking at it, but many still like the convenience and care that comes with traditional mail. What will work best may come only after consulting others on campus or trying both. A related medium much discussed by audience members at a recent NCHC conference session is Facebook. Whether this tool can effectively reach all alumni, who have to become members, or whether it could serve as a supplementary means of communication, remains to be seen.

A second, increasingly popular way to communicate with alumni is through the program website. The first step is to ensure that the website has a separate alumni page and that "alumni" is a prominent tab or menu item among other constituent subjects such as "prospective students" or "faculty." As with all web pages, attractiveness of design and ease of navigability are critical. The alumni web page or pages can offer

- greetings from the director or dean;
- links to news stories about the program and its faculty and students;
- description of the alumni organization (if one exists) and a list of members and officers identified by year of graduation;
- calendar of events for the program (with an open invitation) and of events designed specifically for honors alumni;
- accounts of events, with photographs, such as a homecoming gathering or a recent appearance on campus by an alum;

- announcements of alumni award winners, with photos and profiles, and a nomination form;
- encouragements to become involved with the current program; and
- information about ongoing funds or special fundraising projects and how to make a donation, perhaps including a link to the institution's foundation or development site for on-line credit-card donations.

At the very least a copy of the mailed newsletter should appear on the website as well. A more sophisticated and interactive alumni site might offer a blog or a message board where alumni can post queries.

A periodic survey of alumni is yet another way to maintain contact, find out what alumni valued in their honors experience, and generate interest that could eventually motivate donations. The first alumni survey requires much thought, and perhaps advice from social science faculty as well, because being able to use the same survey again will enable longitudinal comparisons. The survey should elicit both quantifiable responses and open comments, as in teaching evaluations and other assessment instruments. Alumni will generally respond well without the need for anonymity. After the analysis and report of the results, each individual response can go to that alum's folder. Attitudes of alumni toward the program will provide clues about who might be likely prospects for fundraising.

Finally, one-on-one correspondence with alumni can cement relationships and abet fundraising efforts. Directors should show a personal interest in the success of alumni, all the more so if they had a personal relationship with the alumni when they were students, by congratulating them on their accomplishments with a short note or e-mail. My initial interest in several alumni has led to being placed on their e-mail message list; I now receive news of their latest performance, exhibit, degree, job opportunity, or international travel. I always respond personally to these announcements. Faculty, especially thesis advisors, can also help keep track of alumni and stay in contact with them personally.

Using these various forms of communication may very well place honors ahead of the disciplinary departments and colleges. The latter do not often have the time for the personal touch—typical of honors—that treats both current students and alumni as individuals. Thus one of the barriers to fundraising many honors deans and directors have cited— competition with other academic units for overlapping alumni as potential donors—may begin to fall. Now, or in fact simultaneously with communication efforts, the director can invite alumni to honors events and plan special occasions for them.

Events

What are some of the obvious choices for events that honors alumni, particularly those within reasonable driving distance, might be interested in attending? One such event is the major annual honors ceremony, usually held to recognize graduating seniors, to present awards, or to showcase thesis research. Freshman orientations or study abroad information meetings are other likely events. We recently added a music recital and an art show. The alumni newsletter and web page can notify alums of the year's calendar of events. If an alumni organization already exists, its members should take a special interest in attending honors events. Seeing proud students and program quality in person cements alumni relations and inspires alumni toward greater involvement, through time or donations.

Mere attendance, however, is only a minimal goal. If the recognition ceremony includes a meal, directors should ask alumni and faculty as well to sponsor a student's meal. This small contribution can defray expenses, assuming that the honors budget would normally cover the honored student's meal, if not those of their guests. I have known alumni to sponsor up to three students in this way. The program of a major ceremony can include a segment for honoring one or more alumni with an award for their career achievement or for their service to the program. An alum could also be the keynote speaker for the occasion or say a few words at the very least, welcoming seniors to the ranks of proud graduates and encouraging them to stay in touch and give back to the program. For this latter role the president or chair of the honors alumni organization would be particularly appropriate.

Alumni can be engaged during other occasions as well. If honors requires a summer reading assignment for incoming students and breaks them into discussion groups at orientation, directors could invite an alum or two to participate as leaders or discussants, especially if their career expertise touches on the subject of the reading. A research forum will impress alumni with the quality of student work and will perhaps motivate them to become financial supporters of future student research, whether for scholarships, expenses incurred in the work (especially for the arts), or conference travel. A scholar-alum could also speak at a research day. One small honors program invites alumni to judge senior project presentations for prizes. We invited appropriate alumni to be judges in awarding prizes for our art show.

Student service activities such as Relay for Life, housing or ecosystem rehabilitation, or tutoring are other opportunities to engage alumni. Alumni could perform alongside students in a musical showcase or poetry reading, including a marathon recitation of, for example, Homer's *Odyssey*, as in some honors programs. Less ceremonial events to which alumni can make a strong contribution are meetings for majors or clusters of majors, such as English or other humanities majors ("What can you do with a liberal arts degree?"), pre-medicine majors, or professional majors such as journalism or business. Students respond with considerable interest to an alum or a panel of alumni experienced in the field who can give them sound advice as they prepare to launch their careers. I have seen them flock around such guests at the conclusion of a presentation, bubbling with questions. Such experiences are good for the students, of course, but they are also gratifying to the alumni and encourage continuing connectedness to the program. Any event at which alumni can talk with current students is desirable.

More focused efforts are special events planned primarily for alumni. In the beginning stages of alumni relations a common approach is to hold an event for honors alumni in conjunction with the institution's homecoming celebration. This could be a special booth in the alumni association's tent, a lunch between parade and football game, a tailgate party, or a reception at the honors facility before the game. Our own alumni chapter took root at a homecoming ice cream social with students and at the next year's follow-up gathering in our center the morning of homecoming to see who would be interested in starting an organization. Other on-campus alumni events could include a program anniversary celebration, an honors residence hall reunion, or a gathering for certain class years or clusters of years.

If the honors program is located in or near a major population center with a significant number of its alumni living nearby, an alumni "re-connect" reception in a convenient location might work. It could be held at happy hour during the work week or on a Saturday. Alumni usually prefer to devote weekends to family, even though at quitting time during the week they may also be reluctant to delay getting home to their families. Trial-and-error or consultation with the alumni relations office may help determine the best time and location. One promising strategy is to find an alum who is willing to host such a reception at his or her workplace or home; a few current students should be invited as well just to chat with individual alumni or to make a brief presentation. In some cases a presentation by the president or provost or by an interesting honors faculty member can serve as an attraction.

Such receptions can also be planned for other cities where alumni reside. One obvious choice is the annual NCHC conference; I have often invited alumni living in the conference city to an informal gathering at the hotel or a nearby bar. Planning such a reception requires at least two months' lead time. The alumni office or development office can provide names and contact information for honors alumni living in the conference city. The director can then call or write to them to invite them and to ascertain their interest. Such gatherings, even dinner, need not be costly; alumni should pay their own way. If the institution has an organized alumni group in that city, it may help in planning and publicizing the gathering.

In all of these events, directors can choose whether or not to call attention to fundraising projects. At the least such occasions afford the opportunity to exchange news—to share good stories about the program and its students and to show interest in, and catch up with, alumni careers. Alumni also relish the opportunity to see their former honors professors, so faculty should be invited. Again, the stronger honors relations with alumni are, the more likely the alumni are to become donors. As alumni get to know each other through such events, they may also be more likely to join an alumni council.

Organization

At some point directors may feel ready to organize an alumni council. To be viable, such an organization needs a cadre of interested alumni within reasonable driving distance who would be willing to plan activities and meet at least two to four times a year. Before formally instituting such an organization, directors and honors staff members may have noted certain alumni who have attended various events and who have expressed interest in supporting the program or connecting with other alumni. Directors can begin with a small informal group and engage them in helping to plan some alumni events. Such a group may even take the form of a think tank for directors to consult for advice about the program without being constituted as an advisory board. Organizing alumni should occur organically. Formal organization will depend on a dedicated group of at least 8–10 volunteers and a larger pool of interested parties who might not become officers or attend meetings regularly but who still wish to participate.

The next question is whether the institution's alumni relations office has a framework and guidelines for the formation of such groups. For example, does the group need to have bylaws and a strategic plan? The group may be able to design its own organization independently—honors folks are always drawn to nonconformity—but it will need to ascertain the relative advantages of coming under a larger alumni umbrella. Will official recognition for the organization elicit any funding from the central office? Will it gain by having a liaison from that office become a functioning member? Will the alumni office offer helpful advice based on long experience? Will honors gain easier access to alumni publications, listserves, and databases? Policies often change through the years. At one time our alumni office provided a liaison but no funding, then it funded our annual newsletter, then it stopped funding that and supported events only through advance loans. Some alumni offices will not fund an event unless it is designed primarily for alumni, not for alumni and students.

In whatever form an honors alumni organization takes, it can generate useful initiatives. Its members can organize alumni events, with the director's consultation. Their critiques can improve the alumni web pages. They can create alumni awards and select the recipients. They can initiate an honors scholarship for children or relatives of honors alumni and raise money for it. Dedicated leaders and officers are the key. Their energy often sustains the organization. After several years, the current and former officers provide a doubly strong core of committed members. A student liaison or two would also be useful. Attendance at meetings and activities may rise and fall, some members may drop out, and not every idea will work. Quarterly Saturday morning meetings, always with refreshments, worked well for us. Engaging alumni with current students on a service project was successful. Of course, some initiatives faltered, or faltered even after being repeated successfully for several years. Directors must be active in identifying recent alumni in the area to recruit to the group and must attend all meetings to provide updates about the program.

Depending on the size of the program and time commitments of staff members, directors may assign coordination of alumni relations to a staff person. Directors burdened with curriculum and advising duties, teaching, correspondence, and even fundraising will need help. They may have to make the case to the administration that an additional staff position is needed to launch or expand alumni relations and, accordingly, fundraising efforts, in hopes of gaining significant improvements for the program. The administration may prefer that such activities be coordinated by the central alumni and development offices. If little has been done by these offices for honors in the past, directors can argue that they are better positioned to take on these initiatives within a partly decentralized model. Honors has a body of loyal alumni ripe for engaging as donors.

Solicitation

At any point in the development of alumni relations, fundraising can rear its ugly head—er, I mean, arise as a natural opportunity for alumni to support the honors program. As mentioned earlier, various communications can tell alumni how to contribute. Directors can bless the alums' desire to establish an alumni scholarship and help them raise funds for it. If the institution has a tradition of class gifts, honors could start a parallel tradition, starting with new graduates. Or, through personal invitations, several key alums, designated "class captains," might come forward to raise funds among their graduation cohort. Naturally, they should discuss with directors the sort of gift that would leave a legacy with the honors program and be recorded on a plaque displayed in the honors facility. Class reunions or five-year cluster reunions also offer opportunities for fundraising. If honors has a memorial scholarship for a deceased former student or faculty member, some alumni will doubtless have known the person; directors should inform them of the fund's existence and of the benefits it is providing for current and future students. If remodeling, expanding, or constructing anew the honors center is in the offing, directors should launch a significant campaign among alumni to help achieve the goal. Major construction costs, if not covered wholly by the institution, must doubtless come from a major donor or set of key donors with major gifts. Directors can, however, also give alumni, through smaller gifts, a chance to feel a part of the collective effort to bring such a project to fruition. Whether it is purchasing a brick or other piece—whether a souvenir of the former space or a part of the new space—or simply having a name on a plaque, directors can acknowledge contributions at various levels. Later in this chapter I will describe a specific alumni project available to all honors programs: thesis sponsorships.

Two cautions are in order. First, before soliciting any alumni, directors must check with the development office to see if any of them are already being approached for major gifts to other programs. Honors should not interfere with that process with yet another request, or the prospects will think that the university is sending mixed signals or does not coordinate its fundraising internally. Second, directors must use careful judgment in suggesting amounts to contribute or setting amount levels for various recognitions. Although honors students usually go on to successful careers, they do not always attain huge salaries even over time (after all, many of them become academics!). Of course, asking too little is unwise if more is possible. Unless the plan is to segment the solicitation to donors of a certain age range with presumed giving power appropriate for their career point, the solicitation should suggest a range of giving or set a basic price, such as for a brick or a thesis sponsorship, low enough to accommodate those with little means. No one wants to insult alumni by requiring a minimum gift of too high an amount; that approach will encourage many of them to laugh cynically and jettison the solicitation in the circular file. In addition to suggesting various levels, perhaps with honorific titles, directors can set a base price and then list higher levels for optional additional gifts. (See the thesis sponsorship reply form in Appendix C.)

If the solicitation asks for a specific amount, it should not be undermined by a suggestion that gifts in any amount will be happily accepted. Such an explicit statement lets the donor off the hook. Of course, directors will happily accept a smaller donation; they should just not say so in advance! For all of these modest solicitations, they should remember that small donors may become big ones over time if directors treat them graciously.

In alumni solicitations as well as in all those discussed further in this handbook, the message should include a reference to possible matching donations from the donor's employer; many employers give a matching amount, and some give two or three times what the employee donated. In some cases the donor will send employer paperwork for the director to sign, attesting to the receipt of the gift, but often this form must be signed by a foundation official.

Reliance on alumni does not have to stop with personal donations. Many of them will have corporate employers who could become not just matching donors but interested supporters in their own right. The director should seek this additional help from alumni by providing them with materials about the program to share with their employers as they pursue corporate support on behalf of honors. Again, clearance from the development office is necessary. Some young alumni may not be financially capable of a significant donation, but their recent memories of their honors experience and their energy and enthusiasm can be harnessed to persuade their company to take an interest in the program, or at least to move a step closer by agreeing to a meeting with the director and the alumni volunteer who broached the topic.

Concluding this section is a story from an honors director at a large public university about an alumni campaign to endow a scholarship:

> Several years ago I decided it was a good idea to establish an Honors Alumni Endowment. In 2003 the College hired a development officer and the Honors Program made use of her. I gave her names, email addresses, and phone numbers of alumni who had given gifts in the past. She went to work setting up breakfasts, lunches, etc. I went with her to meet with these alumni. We talked about their experiences in the Honors Program and the Development Office "closed the deal." We raised about $25,000 and established the endowment. Unfortunately, the development

officer left the university, so we were left without the help. I've gone about other ways to increase the funding for this account.

Not everyone is lucky enough to have such assistance from a development officer, but even in this case the notoriously high turnover of such staff people can be frustrating. This honors director is resourceful enough to pick up the slack and continue the effort to expand the endowment. Because development officers come and go, directors will benefit from having established their own close relationship with honors alumni.

By whatever means possible, establishing an alumni donor base is critical to successful fundraising overall. Yes, some honors directors may have had the extraordinary good luck of having the president land a hefty donor endowment for the program. Assuming that the institution allows directors to engage in any sort of fundraising at all, however, they will also need to formulate a strategic development plan of their own rather than rely on occasional windfalls. As directors set out to do so, alumni can be their best friends.

Stewardship 101: Effective Written Communications

Now the donations are coming in. Or perhaps directors inherited some donors from their predecessors. Naturally they are grateful for this generous support. Now they must show appreciation by writing prompt thank-you letters and tending to ongoing donor relations. Donors' philanthropic motives are enhanced when directors express gratitude and keep the donors informed about the purposes served by their gifts. Good stewardship means, above all, using donors' gifts in the way they were intended, taking good care of these precious donations, and having integrity in fundraising. It means adhering to donors' desires for confidentiality and even anonymity, if that is their choice.

Good stewardship also means showing appreciation to donors on an ongoing basis. Most donors are modest, but some desire, expect, or even demand recognition. How to recognize donors at various levels of giving often depends on institutional policy, so the director must consult the development office for guidelines and advice. Major gifts may come with naming opportunities, which can be complicated and which may shift over time; they require cooperation with the development staff or upper administration. This first chapter, however, focuses on stewardship fundamentals that apply to all levels of giving. Good stewardship is usually expressed through effective communications, through formal and informal events, and through donor recognition. The latter two will be covered in "Stewardship 301" in the next chapter. Here the focus will be on communications, especially correspondence, both process and content.

Procedures

Surely all of our mothers taught us that whenever someone gives us something we should say "thank you." When I became honors dean, I made it a rule to write a thank-you letter for every gift, whether a check for $5.00 or a $10,000 pledge over five years, whether a faculty member's donation of books to the honors library or a local bank's underwriting of the honorarium for a guest speaker. The institution's foundation will also doubtless send a "form" thank-you, but the director's letter will carry more weight because it comes directly from the program the donor chose to support. It can also be more personal. Some deans of academic colleges make a practice of sending a thank-you only to donors of at least $500 or $1,000. Writing thank-yous for every gift adds labor, but not every letter has to be unique. The director can compose a standard letter for gifts for a certain purpose up to, say, $500, and use it for six months or a year before revising and updating it. Upon receipt of a gift notice, a secretary can print this letter out routinely with a personalized inside address and salutation ready for the director's signature.

Directors should never send an impersonal, unsigned thank-you letter, especially not a printed form. They should never use e-mail in place of a letterhead message that bears an actual signature in blue ink. Larger gifts will demand a fresh letter each time. Using a mixture of approaches, directors can still acknowledge every gift without consuming an excessive amount of time. No matter how minor the gift appears in the overall honors operation, expressing gratitude directly and personally will mean more to the donor and encourage repeated and increased giving in the future.

Here is a case in point: One of my alums found my thesis sponsorship project attractive one year and adopted a thesis student. She received prompt thank-yous from me and the student and, at the end of the school year, a copy of our thesis profile booklet, which included a reference to her gift. The next year she adopted three students. For the two years following, she sent checks for $1,000 aside from the adoption program. Within another year, she and her husband had dedicated a $100,000 endowment to an honors scholarship! This case was unusual but at the very least small donors will often renew their gift year after year.

A similar success story about the value of good stewardship comes from another honors dean, this time involving students much more heavily in the stewardship:

We have a very good relationship with a couple who prefer to fund, in their words, "quirky" things. Indeed, they fund the travel and expenses of the students we bring to the NCHC conference. During a pre-conference meeting before we took the very first group of funded students to the conference, I suggested that we (all) should find a way to thank our benefactors. One of my students recalled that in high school, they had sent postcards to folks who had helped his class go on a trip. "Postcards from Honors" was thus conceived. Every year, each student is required to send a postcard to our good friends who sponsor the trip—they buy and write the postcards, we supply the address and stamps. The first year the postcards (20 or so that year I believe) arrived at the donors' house over the few days immediately after a significant (six-figure) proposal from the Honors College arrived there. Needless to say, the proposal was fully funded and now, six or so years later, their house is full of postcards. Our President held a reception at their house last spring—every surface of their living room and dining room was covered with postcards from Honors. Their giving to the University (almost all through Honors) recently went over the $1,000,000 mark. (In a subsequent communication this dean noted that this couple's annual support will be funded in perpetuity through a $1.2+ million bequest.)

Directors must not hesitate to ask students to write thank-you messages. Their voices will probably mean more than those of administrators. Many institutions and some honors directors now require students to write a thank-you note if their scholarship comes from a private donor; the financial aid office often withholds the scholarship money until the student completes the task.

Above all, directors must express gratitude promptly. If the donation comes directly to the honors office, the thank-you should go out within the week—in fact, as soon as possible. If notice of the gift comes from the foundation office, typically in monthly or weekly (or ideally daily) reports, directors should respond especially quickly because more time has elapsed since the donor's original mailing. Prompt replies show attentiveness, and paying attention is typical of honors folks: paying close attention to students, faculty, staff, alumni, and friends is one of the things we do best.

Content

What goes into a good thank-you letter? Sincerity of tone and freshness of language. Speaking from the heart. No bureaucratic or business jargon. Until directors master the skill, they should test their drafts with honors staff and with development office staff. They should consider the advice of these colleagues but remember that they are expressing their own personality and their honors culture, which is likely to be a bit different from institutional or professional development staff culture. The content of the letter consists of at least three parts. It begins with a direct expression of gratitude for the gift, explicitly acknowledging its amount and purpose. Restating these facts reassures donors that the gift has been accurately recorded and that directors understand the purpose for which the gift is to be used. If this is a repeat gift, the letter should acknowledge that loyalty and commitment. If the gift represents a significant increase, directors may want to acknowledge that, too, with special pleasure.

The main body of the letter should describe the impact of the gift or the specific benefits the gift provides for the program and hence its students. The letter should help donors visualize the actual outcome of their philanthropic impulse—how the money is being put to work for the good of the cause. If, for example, the contribution goes to an unrestricted foundation account, often called a discretionary fund, directors should cite several examples of how they used this fund to support projects otherwise difficult or impossible to accomplish. They might have used such a fund to pay for several students to present at research conferences in the past year. Perhaps they chartered a bus for a class field trip or for a student group's service project an hour's drive from campus. If the contribution enhances the general scholarship fund, the letter can refer to the benefits of having renewable scholarships when recruiting new students, or to the gratification of awarding a special scholarship to an international student to prevent the student's having to drop out and return home.

The heart of the letter should not convey simply a boilerplate news update on the program. The content should relate specifically to the purpose of the gift. If directors wish to communicate to the donor some exciting news, because it will affirm the overall program quality as an incentive to keep investing in it, they should place it separately in a third paragraph. The language in this second paragraph should also connect the purposes for which the gift was used to the strategic priorities of the program. Directors need to show why it is important to honors education to be able to send a biology student to a conference to present his or her thesis research, or to take an honors art history class to a museum, or to ensure that a Ukrainian business major remains part of the program.

The brief closing paragraph repeats the thank-you in different phrasing and affirms the importance of donors such as the reader to the health of the program and to the success of its students. If directors have established an ongoing, more personal relationship with the donor, they may wish to offer seasonal wishes (e.g., for an interesting new year) or regards to the spouse, or they might refer to an upcoming event at which they expect to see the donor in person. They may wish to refer to an enclosure that they think will be of interest, such as a student's conference report, a story in the campus newspaper, or an honors giveaway such as a bookmark or brochure, especially if the item is related to the purpose of the gift. One caveat: Because the letter will document a tax deduction for the donor, the amount of the gift listed should not include any quid pro quo benefits. For example, if the donor paid $150 for a scholarship dinner that cost $25 for food, the actual gift is just $125. Or the letter can acknowledge the total amount but indicate clearly what part is a tax-deductible contribution.

Here are two sample thank-you letters, one for a general fund and another for a special-purpose fund.

April 27, 200_

Mr. Brian Brain
Address
City, State, Zip

Dear Brian,

Thank you so much for your generous donation of $___ to the Honors College Dean's Discretionary Fund! Your support of the Discretionary Fund allows me to address the greatest needs of the College and fund projects beyond our normal budget capacity.

Thanks to this fund, I was able to support several students to attend conferences and field experiences this year. Several accompanied us to the national and regional honors conferences, and one thesis student was able to present his research at an international biology conference. Three musical theatre majors participated in very successful New York Spring Showcase auditions, and another theatre student participated in the national Black Theatre Association fringe festival. A thesis student in early childhood education is also receiving support for an intersession research trip to Italy in May. The fund also helps cover transportation costs for our spring break restoration project at a Hurricane Katrina site in Mississippi.

One of the most interesting uses of the fund has been to purchase art work from graduating art majors to display in the Honors Center. In fact, we are commissioning a piece for our reception area wall this spring.

Again, we are grateful for your thoughtful contribution to the ambitious work being done by our students. It has enriched our program.

Sincerely,

Sam

Samuel Smarts, Dean

Note that the opening line calls the donation "generous" no matter how small the gift. Any giving is generous, so even if directors think that a supposedly affluent donor should make more than a token contribution, they must be gracious; they do not know what other competition exists for that person's resources. That opening line also needs to convey some sincere emotion. The plentiful concrete examples of the gift's use, although still without individual students' names, provide reassuring evidence. In this example, directors might choose to omit the mention of the office art if they suspect that that is a less than universally acceptable use of this fund, or they could explain further how it celebrates student work and offers compensation for students whose field is poorly rewarded financially.

April 27, 200_

Ms. Clara Clever
Address
City, State, Zip

Dear Clara,

Thank you so much for your contribution of $___ to our University Honors Program Scholarship Fund! Your generosity is helping to provide renewable scholarships to our incoming students, thus enhancing our ability to recruit outstanding young scholars to Honors. Given budget constraints and the increasing financial burden of a college education, your gift will make a real difference for our students.

Here are some of the new students who are benefiting from our freshman scholarships:

- A journalism major who in his first year has already become a designer for the campus newspaper;
- A young woman from Bosnia and another from Ukraine;
- A young bassoonist who began his XXU career while still a high school student and who is taking a 22-credit-hour load and performing in four ensembles;

- A young woman with a boundless intellectual curiosity whose interests range from education and science to conservation, Swahili, and African dance;

- A young woman in biology/pre-med already active in Habitat for Humanity, the International Film Society, and the Medical Students Association, who has just spent four months teaching basic computer skills to residents in a retirement home, and whose twin brother is an Honors meteorology major.

The scholarship fund also provides support for participation in life-changing off-campus programs such as the Washington Internship Program and study abroad programs that help make our students citizens of the world (check out some of their reactions on our website: http://www.xx.edu/honors/studyabroad). We are proud of the ambitious students who undertake these special learning experiences and wish to do our best to support them in their quest.

Again, we are deeply grateful to you for contributing to our educational mission with your gift.

Sincerely,

Wanda

Wanda Wise, Director

Here, the strategic goal of recruiting top students signals the importance of the gift. The bullet list offers an alternative for listing examples that may be easier to digest than the solid prose paragraph in the first letter. The reference to the website functions not only to provide more examples of the benefits of scholarship support but may lure the donor into browsing other pages of the website. An alternative would have been to enclose a single sheet of student testimonials with the thank-you letter. Both letters use first names in the salutation and signature lines. This choice is partly a matter of individual judgment, but I would recommend this friendly approach even for donors the director does not know personally. Both letters doubtless contain ideas or word choices that would not suit some directors. Each director must find his or her own voice and engage readers in a direct, dignified, down-to-earth, and human way.

Other important stewardship communications are publications, newsletters, DVDs, brochures, and invitations. Why are these important for stewardship? Most of these items will reaffirm the value of honors as a cause worth supporting. They put a specific face on the program, especially when they tell individual stories and display photographs of students and faculty in action. In this way effective public relations tools support fundraising. As alumni become donors, for example, the alumni newsletter serves the double function of keeping them informed about the good things happening in honors and inspiring them to continue to support the program financially. Directors should regularly send a major production, such as a creative writing magazine or a thesis profile book, to major (primarily endowment) donors as a courtesy, with a cover letter sharing their pride in their students and expressing gratitude again for the donor's support. Some programs design a special newsletter or brochure just for donors as a sign of special attention. In one case I sent a documentary video made by a class to a few donors who I knew would be interested not only in the subject but also in the independent and creative spirit of the students. If the program has a new recruiting brochure or DVD, that can provide yet another opportunity to maintain contact with a major donor; a short cover letter should accompany its mailing.

Active and ongoing contact with major donors is a basic principle of Stewardship 101. This was another lesson of unintended consequences that I learned as a novice dean. When I took office, I found out that our college had received several memorial scholarship endowments some years earlier. Contact with the donors had been intermittent. I wrote to the donors to introduce myself and to express gratitude for their gifts. I also mentioned points of pride about their scholarship recipients. At the time, my purpose was common courtesy; I was not thinking that additional donations might be forthcoming. In one case we were soon able to have lunch with one donor, her sibling contributors, and the student recipient. This donor thereafter made the first of her annual additional gifts to the endowment, and I wrote a warm thank-you letter. The next year this donor told me how pleased she was with how we used the endowment and how we kept in touch with her—that in fact we were much better stewards than another institution that had also benefited from her philanthropy. As our encouraging attentiveness—personalized thank-you letters, publications, holiday cards, occasional coffee or lunch—continued over the years, her annual gifts expanded the endowment principal so that the scholarship she had designated also grew in size for the recipients.

Here is a final stewardship story from a director of a small honors program:

> Our development office offered to assign a small endowment to the program, assuming I'd be willing to meet with the benefactor. I have met with him several times and will speak with him on the phone several times a year. I also make sure that he is

informed about our activities and how we use the proceeds from his endowment—for example, we used some money from the proceeds of the endowment to purchase books for our book club. The students who received the books sat in my office and wrote thank-yous. He then sent me a check to replace the cost of the books. I never "asked" for money, but the communication with him provided him with the motivation and the opportunity to offer it. He said something to me once that I think is very important: "I just want someone to pay a little attention." The mistake we sometimes make is forgetting that there is someone behind each donation.

Here the students' participation in stewardship warmed the heart of the donor to the point of replacing the endowment funds used for the book purchase, in effect making an additional donation.

Good stewardship is common courtesy, but it also pays off in the long run in directors' increased comfort level with fundraising and in donor confidence expressed through additional contributions.

Securing the Support of Top Administrators

Honors plays a valuable role in the institution and furnishes student "points of pride" for presidents and provosts to highlight in speeches about academic excellence. Of course, this role is seldom recognized or valued as much as directors could wish. Honors deans and directors come and go, but sometimes presidents and provosts come and go even more frequently. Their familiarity with the honors program's tradition of excellence and their budgetary support can be fragile. The degree to which top administrators think of honors when they engage in fundraising varies considerably. They may also establish or follow policies about who is allowed to do fundraising, policies that may exclude honors leaders and that may need to be addressed. Personal, historical, or political tensions may also exist between honors and the central administration. NCHC lore is rife with stories of the fickleness of administrative support and encouragement, stories even of administrators who wish to eliminate honors entirely.

If the current relations between the honors program and top administrators are uncomfortable or administrators' view of honors is unknown, directors should approach better-positioned colleagues for information and advice. Whether directors have inherited tensions or discovered them, they need to address them. They should find out what they can do to resolve such tensions or whether they will have to live with them. A dean or another middle administrator may be a useful ally. One honors program was saved by an arts and sciences dean who defended the program to a new president, who was contemplating eliminating it. But that is an extreme case. More likely is the problem of indifference or ignorance, especially if directors do not report directly to the provost's or academic vice president's office.

The person to whom directors do report directly needs to be their ally and advocate, not just their boss and judge. If it is a dean, directors need to ensure that they have that person's support and understanding, through periodic face-to-face meetings, written updates, annual reports, and a stream of good news. With that dean's knowledge and blessing, they should meet with the provost and president personally from time to time to keep honors on their radar screens. If directors report to the provost or associate provost, they will supply the same reporting and public relations documents and also meet personally on a periodic basis. In such a case they may have easier access to the president as well. If they are deans, they will probably be better known and more visible to the upper administration, including all vice presidents.

No matter what the reporting line is, directors should keep the president and provost well informed about what honors is doing, especially through publications and through periodic points of pride as they occur. These top officers should be on regular honors mailing lists for newsletters and show-and-tell student products. Directors should ascertain whether they are receptive to email or always need paper communications. I was pleasantly surprised when, at an out-of-state institutional recruiting reception, our new president departed from script and read aloud a thesis abstract from our thesis profile booklet, saying, "This is what you can do if you come to Kent State." I had just sent it to him a week earlier. Directors should also invite these chief administrators to major honors events, such as annual graduation or awards ceremonies or a research forum, where they can speak or present faculty or student awards. Directors should treat them as special guests by means of a cordial invitation, personal greeting, shepherding to reserved seating when they arrive at the event, and public acknowledgment from the dais of their support of honors.

Most relevant to fundraising is to keep honors at the forefront of administrators' awareness as one of the institution's best embodiments of academic excellence. Directors can furnish them with statistics and with vivid, individual anecdotes of student achievement that they can tout not only in recruiting speeches but also in fundraising conversations with major donor prospects. Administrators are aware that academic excellence is the heart of the institution's mission. Athletics or campus buildings may be important to some donors and may be fundraising priorities, but administrators must always be armed with impressive information about the learning experiences of students. Whether the president does most or all of a small college's fundraising or plays a significant role in a large university's pursuit of donors at the million-dollar level, he or she will want any good stories honors directors can provide. The president and provost also need to be armed with justifications for the existence of honors—on their own or reminded by directors—in case they encounter donor prospects who are skeptical and see honors as elitist. Even if the institution places major responsibility for fundraising on the directors' shoulders, directors should also find fundraising allies in the president and provost, who have significant fundraising responsibility for the institution as a whole or particularly for academic affairs. Directors must be aware of any policies or procedures for shared responsibility for fundraising and make sure that they have the blessing of top administrators for their own fundraising plans and priorities.

Getting to Know the Development Office

When an institution has a development office and fundraising is not simply a function of the president's office, development operations are usually headed by a high-level administrator, a director or a vice president of institutional advancement or of university relations and development, which may or may not also include communications and marketing. A highly centralized fundraising model locates all development activity and coordination in this institutional development office. A highly decentralized model locates the largest responsibility in individual academic or athletic units, which have their own support staff working under academic leaders such as deans and school directors. A third model divides the labor between a central office and individual units with constituent development officers; in this mixed model the central office can coordinate institution-wide fundraising projects, capital campaigns, prospect research, and the annual fund. The central office may also partially fund and share supervision of the constituent development officers.

If directors are new to honors or are just turning their attention to fundraising, they will need to ascertain the development model currently in operation at the institution. How does honors fit into the scheme? Are development staff members aware of honors? Has honors been listed as a destination for donations in the annual campaign, in capital campaigns, in faculty/staff campaigns, in planned giving? If not, why not? Who decides on institutional fundraising priorities? Are there resources, such as a library, to guide someone new to fundraising? Do the academic degree-granting colleges have development officers? These are some of the questions directors should ask key people in the development structure. They should start by making sure that the vice president or director in charge knows who they are and why the honors program is worth fundraising effort. Depending on the size of the development staff, they may be meeting with coordinators of such areas as major gifts, the annual fund, planned giving, corporate and foundation giving, capital campaign, constituent development officers, research, and donor relations. Directors should also find out who the constituent development officers are and probe what it would take to get their attention through shared interests.

From the development vice president, directors can gain a sense of the big picture—the structural model used, the availability of budget to support fundraising activities, the status of any capital campaign planned or in progress, the role of top administrators in fundraising, and the general giving capacity of the institution's alumni, business community, and region. In turn directors can convey the value and importance of honors and keep this vice president well informed of honors achievements on an ongoing basis. From each of the other staff members, directors can learn valuable information and advice and in turn make that person much more aware of honors. In terms of the annual fund, they can determine whether telephone or direct mail works better. If there is a phone center, they can learn how it can or does target honors alumni specifically. They can ask to come to the phone center in person to give a pep talk to the student callers and highlight fundraising priorities. They can learn from a major gifts officer what goes into an endowment agreement, and they can obtain a template to examine. Similarly, they can learn much about policies and procedures for planned giving, corporate and foundation solicitation, and prospect research.

In talking to constituent development officers, directors should acknowledge that honors has alumni in common, but they should encourage collaboration as opposed to competition in seeking what the donor is most interested in supporting. They should point out that fundraising for scholarship support offers an especially fruitful opportunity for cooperation. They may find a donor interested in supporting a student in biology with a scholarship; they would disburse the scholarship fund, but they would probably have to engage the biology department in the selection process and that department's student would benefit. Conversely, the constituent development officer in, say, education, now knowledgeable about honors, might secure a scholarship endowment for an honors education major because honors membership assures the donor that a top student would be selected as the recipient. Education would control the fund, but the honors director would be involved in the selection process and an honors student would benefit.

In an unusual case of paying attention to the development office, one university honors director had discovered from reading foundation reports that a number of institution-wide, endowed scholarships were not being awarded because the small development staff did not have the time to find students who matched the donors' wishes. A good entrepreneur, she volunteered to manage about ten of them, amounting to $20,000 annually. She awarded them to honors students in their ninth semester, thus relieving the development office of embarrassment, pleasing the donors, and serving her own students who had exhausted all other scholarship support.

The goal in these efforts is to learn as much as possible from development staff, to teach them as much as possible about honors, and to address gaps in institutional fundraising that have negatively affected honors. Directors may wish to ask that honors be added to a list of campus-wide programs (e.g., library, graduate program, and athletics) for annual-campaign solicitation. Honors may have been invisible to the staff in planned giving, but directors can make them aware of older honors alumni as well as the attractiveness of honors to prospects who do not know about it but who might enjoy being associated with its quality. One Midwestern honors director made a point of inviting a key person in the central development office to co-present a session at NCHC. The person was suitably impressed by the conference, by honors education, and by the university's own honors students and became an advocate. A similar partisanship can arise from inviting a development staff person to honors events at which students shine. In the case of the decentralized and mixed models of development structure, depending on the size of the honors program and of the development budget, honors directors should feel entitled to representation by a constituent development officer, even if shared with another unit. (Arguing for a development officer will be taken up in Chapter 2.)

Here is a happy story from an honors director at a two-year institution, illustrating how making the central development office aware of honors' needs can have successful results:

> I went to the director of development last fall, told my story, and asked for help—could we try for a donor or a grant to support

enrichment activities—fees, tickets, even just hire a van to go to a place. To my surprise I got a call a month later and was told we were given $2500 by an anonymous donor. Wow! It is great!! Caution. It was apparently a one-time gift and so far no more action has occurred. I guess that honors fundraising was on a checklist and it got its check.

The writer's "caution" deserves to be expanded. The last two sentences indicate that this honors director remains in the dark about the operations of the development office and assumes that honors was simply given "a turn." This director probably does not have the time, or does not feel empowered, to push the process further and follow up on the possibility of continuing cultivation of this or other donors. The director's caveat dampens the elation over the gift. In a subsequent communication this director reports writing a thank-you letter to "an unknown group," accounting for the expenditures, and later discovering the donor's identity by accident. The director continues: "the foundation office continued to be secretive about its methods and priorities. I still don't know why the donor donated at that particular time to our program. We now have a new president who has put a higher value on honors, so I hope the foundation gets the message." My suggestion is not only to seek more information about fundraising processes but also to offer assistance in fundraising for honors.

As a partner to the development office, the institution's foundation is also critical to honors directors. The foundation holds, invests, and disburses donations. It can set up and maintain accounts for honors. Directors should get to know the foundation director and record-keepers and obtain answers to the following questions: What is the spendable endowment interest payout currently and how and when are account statements issued? How much service or maintenance fee is charged on accounts? To support development activities, does the foundation deduct from honors accounts a percentage of each gift honors receives, or only of each gift that the central development office raises for honors through its own efforts? Or does it take deductions only from non-scholarship donations? How much time must pass before usable interest has been generated from a new endowment gift? How much delay is there between a scholarship award through the financial aid and bursar's offices and its actual transfer as an expenditure from the foundation account? Who is the best contact person for information about accounts, and what is the best method, email or a phone call? If account statements are shared only with the director's superior, how can the director also receive them? How can the director transfer funds from one account to another, assuming no restrictions on their use? What is the difference between the book value and the market value of endowments? Directors should not be in the dark about honors foundation accounts or about how the whole fundraising process currently works at the institution.

Developing Modest Projects

Some small fundraising projects were mentioned in the earlier section on filthy lucre and will be expanded here. For what purposes does honors need money? What will private donations enable honors to do for its students beyond its current budget? What are the still unfulfilled priorities in the honors strategic plan? Ideas for fundraising often come from that wish list that directors should always have on hand. This wish list should always represent consultation with staff and advisory committees, it may involve some background work such as student opinion surveys or research on costs, and it should be aligned with overall strategic priorities.

This chapter explores the relatively low-cost items on the wish list, not the multi-million-dollar endowed scholarship program that will be discussed in Chapter 3. The list may contain wishes that cannot come true given the current budget—several new computers, a laser printer, a display case, travel expenses for students presenting at conferences, gift cards for faculty awards, prizes for a thesis competition, a recruiting scholarship for an international student, reimbursement to students for thesis expenses, a joint camping excursion with another honors program nearby, small grants for study abroad. Where can directors find money to enrich the program in these ways?

Directors might occasionally find a donor, especially an alum, who will buy a refrigerator for the kitchen, fund a computer upgrade, or pay for a display case and its installation. Donors will more likely respond to a call for student aid such as prize recognition, research support, and travel support. A local travel agency might put up $300 or $500 to help a student undertake study abroad. A faculty member might pay for a subscription to *The New York Times* for the lounge or library or for a first-year colloquium.

Perhaps the wish list includes care packages for students during finals week, and parents could provide the cost for them. Members of the honors student committee or organization might help make such an appeal, from their own student point of view. Parents might take an interest in other projects that directly affect their children, such as a fund for internship support, study abroad, or renovation of a student lounge. A good habit is writing a welcome letter to parents of incoming students. I also wrote to parents following their child's graduation, congratulating them and soliciting their donations; this effort had limited success, but in other honors programs or institutional cultures it might work. The liberal arts college one of our daughters attended has dunned us annually ever since she graduated 20 years ago. One honors director holds a summer luncheon for parents of incoming students to establish relationships and to plant the seed of philanthropy. Another director hosts a parents' picnic and follows it in two weeks with a solicitation letter.

Speaking of parents as potential donors, a scholarship fund may have special appeal to parents whose children have benefited from an honors scholarship that has relieved both parents and children of some of the cost burden of their education. One honors dean and his development officer send a postcard to all parents, soliciting annual fund support; they follow up with calls from honors students. They also make a more personal appeal to the 10 or 20 parents with the greatest capacity. A number of parents have made four-year pledges equal to the amount of their children's first-year $3500 scholarship. Another dean with only young alumni decided to start fundraising with parents by organizing a parent society, with an attendant website, that looks promising. (See Appendix C for the sign-up form.) Success in fundraising with parents, no matter what the project, depends on their capacity, their perspective on what their child's education is costing them, the institution's tradition of inviting their financial support, the timing of the solicitation, and the degree to which honors directors have persuaded them of the program's quality.

Unless a lead has emerged for one of the modest projects mentioned so far, however, directors should prefer to rely on building an unrestricted or discretionary fund, which they can use to support many small projects. They may think that donors will not give money without a specific purpose earmarked for it in advance. Certainly the national trend has been away from unrestricted giving in favor of an interest in specific projects; however, many sensible donors apprehend that honors needs vary and that directors must have some freedom to judge when and where to spend unrestricted monies. They will trust honors leaders to make responsible choices.

Directors should not think of such a fund as a blank check or slush fund, which connotes untrustworthiness or potential abuse. They should speak of it as a fund that allows them to meet the greatest needs of the program at any given moment. Such needs may include additional filing cabinets, copier repair, emergency student aid, copies of books for required reading for incoming students, or an unexpected increase in postage or supplies—in fact, anything that will aid the program's success. Some honors programs, such as the honors colleges at the University of

South Carolina and the University of Central Arkansas, feed such a general fund through a student matriculation fee, and they accomplish much with it. In such cases directors should feel an obligation to use the fund as directly as possible for students, rather than, say, for equipment that the institution should fund, and to show the students explicitly how it is being used. One dean has the students make up a wish list for how the money should be spent. In several NCHC listserve discussions, however, the majority of respondents have argued that a matriculation fee is for various reasons a bad idea.

Aside from projects from the wish list of small additional items that the budget cannot accommodate, directors can also seek underwriting or sponsorship of costs that normally do come out of the budget, thus freeing the particular budget line for other purposes. If a major recognition event includes a meal, directors can ask faculty and alumni to sponsor a student by covering the cost of the student's meal. For an annual reception for honors faculty, they can seek a local business to underwrite the cost of the food or of the bar. If selling an honors T-shirt makes only a little money over cost, they can seek a donor to cover the cost so that they can pocket all the sales income. Selling honors paraphernalia is generally not much of a moneymaker for either the discretionary fund or the student organization. On the other hand, if the members of the student organization wish to raise funds for the program and not just for their own activities or charitable causes, their creativity and energy may produce some money that can make a difference, especially if honors operates on a small or tight budget.

Here is an obvious small project any honors program can undertake. I have found that one of the easiest and most rewarding ways of securing alumni donors is to ask them to sponsor or adopt a thesis student. In an NCHC listserve survey a few years ago, 70% of respondents reported that the senior thesis was required for graduation with honors. For most deans and directors, this means that all of the honors alumni will be aware of the labor and rewards of completing a thesis and will probably feel a sympathetic connection to current students undertaking the same ambitious work. Although the thesis is optional in my own honors college, we have over a thousand alumni who have completed one. I reported on our "adopt-a-thesis-student" project at NCHC conferences and in the *National Honors Report* in 2001 ("Honors Fundraising: A Story of Adoption," *NHR* 22.2 [Summer 2001]: 7–9). After building the program for a few years, we reached a point at which every one of the annual 50–60 thesis students was sponsored by an alum or donor friend. In our case we had been offering each thesis student a partial reimbursement for thesis expenses up to $75. (Many students submitted receipts for less, some for more, so sometimes we were able to cover more if the expenses were extraordinary.) The adoption fee initially covered this reimbursement. After a generous alum pledged an endowment for thesis fellowships, we raised the reimbursement to $100 and added to the fee a $50 contribution to this fund to expand it. Now the total fee has been raised again to $200. This may seem a small-scale fundraising operation, and the correspondence requires a bit of time, but the reimbursement money generated saved our budget over $5,000 annually, and the extra donations to the fellowship endowment doubled the fund so that it could generate two $1,000 thesis fellowships annually. Most of the sponsors look forward to choosing a new student every year.

What accounts for the success of such a project? Donors of small sums as well as large relish the connection with individual students and a visible result of their contributions. Previous sponsors receive their annual solicitation letter in November with a list of current thesis students, including their majors, advisors, and titles. (See a sample copy, with return form, in Appendix C.) They choose whom they wish to sponsor; sometimes they select as many as three to five, but most usually support one. I write each donor a thank-you letter with FERPA-appropriate information about the student. I write a notice of the sponsorship to the student, including information about the alum's honors thesis, career, and address, along with a request that the student write a thank-you note to the donor. A copy of this letter goes to the student's thesis advisor and department chair. Copies of both letters go into the student's folder and the alum's folder. At the end of the year, a thesis profile booklet acknowledges the sponsors at the front and on each student's page, and the donors receive copies. In February, assuming that some students remain to be adopted, I send the same solicitation to the thesis alumni who have never sponsored a student before, to complete the project. The ability to choose a specific student whose project interests the donor, or who was mentored by the same advisor as the donor was, seems critical. Beyond the thank-you letter, some students send the donor an abstract or even a copy of their completed thesis. Alumni donors respond warmly to this personal connection.

One heartwarming example comes to mind. A young alum, then a Ph.D. student elsewhere, responded to my annual solicitation with regret, saying that although his honors thesis had been critical to his admission to the best doctoral program in the country in his field, he was financially strapped. A month later he wrote back unexpectedly to report that he had just received a small cash prize for outstanding doctoral research. He decided to use it to sponsor a current thesis student after all. And the connection did not end there: after receiving his Ph.D. he returned to our university as a new faculty member and eventually taught an honors course for us.

Some non-alumni friends, including the provost, have also become regular sponsors. One year we succeeded in persuading a local environmental organization to sponsor three biology students doing ecological research. The students presented their results at the group's meeting to the accompaniment of many lively audience questions and comments.

Directors do not have to follow this model exactly when conducting a thesis sponsorship program. If no reimbursement policy is in place, this project can initiate it, perhaps funding it completely through donors. The adoption fee can also be used for other purposes such as conference travel, a thesis forum or exhibition, or a research grant fund. We began to offer the additional option of a straight $500 thesis scholarship, and several alumni responded. Even a small fee could be awarded directly to the student as scholarship aid or as a book award through the campus bookstore. The adoption fee can vary depending on the estimate of what alumni are willing to give, but beginning modestly is probably wise.

Other small projects, such as senior class gifts or support for class field trips, have been mentioned in passing. No matter what projects directors devise in consultation with staff, advisory committee, and perhaps the development office, they should remember again that *starting small is OKAY*. Developing modest projects along with efforts to attract major donors is perfectly acceptable and common. Directors can use all the help they can get.

Exploring Grant Funding

As directors formulate their fundraising strategy, they should investigate corporations and foundations that offer grant support to worthy educational causes. They should consider not only writing their own grant proposals but also collaborating with other units on campus and finding ways to take advantage of others' grants. At the outset they need to be prepared with several attitudes. They need to be realistic in their expectations. They need to be precise in matching their project to the grant-funder's interests. They need to treat the grant-funder with the same respect and candor as they would an individual donor. Finally, they must be willing to devote considerable time to entering into a personal relationship with the grant-funder and to preparing a proposal.

Corporations and foundations have generally not been cash cows for honors programs, and government grants are highly competitive.

Directors can start their exploration by consulting the central development office staff about local, regional, and national foundations—whether family, corporate, or community—particularly if a staff member can focus on these prospects. Chances are that the institution is far ahead of honors directors in pursuing and achieving such support—especially from local foundations—and that directors will need to have a detailed conversation to ascertain whether these prospects might be interested in funding honors and whether, and to which ones, they would be allowed to appeal for support. For large grants only the upper administration and deans of disciplinary units may be allowed to approach such funding sources, and only in carefully orchestrated ways.

Directors should also learn about major government grants, such as those under the U.S. Department of Education under FIPSE (Fund for the Improvement of Post-Secondary Education) or those awarded by the National Science Foundation (NSF), even though the proposal process for these is extremely time consuming and requires collaboration with the campus's external funding office. State humanities and arts councils, as organs of the National Endowment for the Humanities (NEH) or National Endowment for the Arts (NEA), may be more accessible, although their grants are smaller. Some funding sources have a competition with a fixed deadline. Others are open to ongoing discussion and to the development, in guided stages, of a convincing case for support. Many require a financial commitment from the institution or other co-funders. Some simply offer a mission statement and wait for proposals, while others issue requests for proposals (RFPs) that seek solutions to specific problems. More rarely, some foundations accept proposals only by invitation.

As directors become more ambitious, they should consult the most comprehensive resource on grants, the Foundation Directory Online, which is part of the Foundation Center's website at http://foundation center.org. The problem is that this continuously updated and comprehensive source is accessible only by subscription, at various levels, by month or by year. The low monthly charge will be worth paying if directors can accomplish their search in that time period. If the institution subscribes, they may gain access that way. Otherwise, they may wish to consult the Center's regional or local reference collections, usually located in public libraries. Librarians there can be helpful in finding the right keywords to use for the Center's CD catalogs so as to narrow the search more quickly. The institutional library might also house the Center's older selective print catalogs, e.g., *Grants for Higher Education 2003–2004*, which covers most of the 1,000 largest foundations by state. Descriptions of the foundations include purpose, eligibility, and examples of recent grants. Once directors locate a granting source that seems favorable for their purposes, they can search for its website, which will offer additional and more up-to-date details, including instructions for the proposal process. A critical part of the research will be reading about other recent grants by the funder, contacting the recipients personally to ask about their funded projects, and sounding out an appropriate staff member at the granting entity about the appropriateness of the project in mind.

While directors are learning about major national or regional grant funding, they should not neglect sources close to home. At the very least they should be aware of the twice-yearly NCHC Portz Fund grant program. The NCHC website offers information about how to apply and what projects are fundable. Like many such documents, the Portz proposal form asks what funds the institution will be committing to the total budget for the project. These grants are modest (small ones up to $500, large up to $1,000), but they can make a difference to an honors program. Here are some examples of projects funded by the Portz Fund grant program in recent years:

- an oral history project ($500 for equipment and transportation)
- a student-led workshop on resilience for high school students ($479 for books and an online training program)
- a reading program with the author as guest speaker ($400 for the honorarium)
- a student-driven seminar series ($495)
- a service-learning course ($500)
- a faculty retreat ($600 for the speaker honorarium)
- faculty honoraria ($600 matching grant)
- an inaugural campus recycling program ($895)
- equipment for a smart classroom when the institution would not provide it ($1,000 for teaching technology)
- a research assistantship when the institution would not provide any research support ($1,000 as a prompt to the institution)
- two art shows ($500 and $1,000).

These and other grants have been awarded to a wide range of programs at community colleges, church-affiliated colleges, private universities, and large state universities.

Whether directors apply for a Portz grant, corporate funding, a FIPSE or an NSF program award, or a Bill and Melinda Gates grant, they must follow the principles of effective grantsmanship. They may have solid faculty experience in communicating with granting agencies and writing grant proposals for research funding, especially if they are in the sciences, social sciences, engineering, education, or nursing. A disproportionately large number of honors deans and directors, however, come from the humanities. They may be excellent writers, but they probably have far less experience in writing grant proposals because far less government and foundation funding is available to them, and grantsmanship is not a major expectation of them as faculty members as it is for scientists. They probably also shrink from the idea of cultivating personal relationships with staff in the granting agency.

Because most honors directors are fairly new to grant writing as part of fundraising for the honors program, what follows are some basic guidelines to help them feel less daunted by the process. First, as they look at various granting agencies and types of grants, they must study carefully descriptions of the sorts of projects the agencies support and the eligibility guidelines. They will want to make sure that these are a match for the honors program and the projects they hope to fund. Any discrepancy is cause for quick elimination from the competition. If they are unsure about their project's suitability, they should not hesitate to call the agency for clarification. In fact, even if they are confident about the match, they will benefit from making themselves and their intentions known to the granting officer, on the telephone or even better in a face-to-face meeting. They should ask this person for advice about the project concept, take notes on any reactions and suggestions, and use them as they formulate the proposal. Any early investment in the project by this staff person can make directors more successful in securing the grant. Susan Golden, in *Secrets of Successful Grantsmanship: A Guerilla Guide to Raising Money* (San Francisco: Jossey-Bass, 1997) makes a convincing case for the importance of establishing such personal relations before submitting a proposal, except where such contact is explicitly forbidden. She also provides detailed advice about every step in the process of seeking grant support.

As directors look for a likely grant opportunity, they will have in hand a short list of projects drawn from their wish list for which they could use external funding. As one example of a granting agency, the Ohio Humanities Council has a highly informative and useful website (http://www.ohiohumanities.org) that lists, under the tab for "Grant Guidelines," contact information and sections on the following subjects:

Definition of "humanities"

Description of Council

Eligible applicants

Eligible projects

Grant categories

Proposal review process

Reasons for not funding

Application process

Instructions for submitting proposals

Grantee responsibilities

Compliance requirements

Glossary of terms used

Application checklist

Deadlines for drafts & final proposals

Special notes for electronic media proposals

Boxes and sidebars offer highlights, special notes, and examples of funded projects. I quickly learned that (a) mini-grants are available for proposal preparation, say, for the cost of a consultant; (b) honors would need to provide at least matching funds; (c) the project narrative, with its specified seven parts, must not exceed six pages; and (d) I should freely consult with a named staff person at the Council. Other state humanities and arts councils offer similarly useful websites. Many websites and newsletters advertise grants for science and math projects in higher education, often in concert with local schools.

Sometimes reading grant descriptions will give directors an idea for a project that had not occurred to them before. If so, they should be careful not to be too hasty to switch focus. Their wish list should have been carefully thought out, backed by some preparatory work, and supported by strategic priorities. A new project arising simply from the availability of grant support needs to be vetted in a similar way if they wish to push it forward and apply for the grant. Their purpose should drive the grant process, not the other way around. Opportunism may lead them astray from their priorities and even their mission.

After directors have determined that their program and project fit a funding agency's priorities, they must decide whether they or a staff member can take the time and effort to do justice to developing a relationship and writing a proposal. If so, they must plot a realistic timetable that will allow them to meet any deadlines at least two or three weeks early. When they are ready to prepare the written proposal, they should follow the instructions exactly for its structure and content. They should answer directly any questions posed and structure the proposal in exactly the format requested, with transparent headings matching the information desired. Instead of crafting the sections in order, they may wish to start with the implementation and budget sections, which will force them to think through the project in depth before writing the basic description of it. They should cite persuasive facts about the importance and value of the project, the realistic basis for estimating cost and time involved, and the successful track record of the honors program. They need to address such questions as these: How will they measure the effectiveness of their project once it is implemented? What is compelling about their project in terms of the grant-funder's mission? How can it reach readers whose purpose is to try to support such projects? Directors should supply enough concrete detail so that readers can vividly imagine the consequences and significance of the project. A concise, clean style is critical. Directors should note and follow any maximum given for word or page count, as well as requirements for font style and size and any preference for anonymity on the proposal pages themselves. They should be careful not to over-write the information they supply; they should be straightforward and (did I say it before?) *concise*.

Directors should readily seek the help of the institution's grants office and its experts on proposal writing. They should ask others in their office and among their grant-getting faculty to read and critique their drafts. They must proofread extremely carefully, using others' eyes as well as their own. For further reference, they may wish to use the proposal-writing tutorial on the Foundation Center's website or consult practical books such as Golden's, which was cited earlier. Another useful source is The Grant Institute (http://www.thegrantinstitute.com), which offers workshops around the country, as does the Foundation Center, and online resources, for a fee.

When directors happily receive their grant, they should immediately write a thank-you letter. They will want to maintain a long-term relationship with the funder for possible future grants. They will publicize the grant in communications and let their top administrators know about it. They must be good grant administrators, using all of the money to fulfill the purpose for which it was awarded. They must do all that they can to make the project succeed, perhaps by drumming up student attendance at an event or making sure a designated staff member is monitoring the project closely. They must follow any reporting stipulations. Most grantors require a final report, but even if it is not strictly required, a closing document reporting the results of the funded project will be appreciated by the grantor and be useful for honors records and annual reports. If the project extends significantly over time, an interim progress report is in order. Directors must comply with any reporting deadlines.

Aside from direct grants from external agencies, directors can learn to take advantage of any grants received by others at their institution. An obvious choice is faculty or department research grants that include funding for undergraduate students. Many NSF grants now have this enrichment of undergraduate learning as a stipulation. Some of these may be multidisciplinary as well, with opportunities for a variety of majors to become involved in a high-level project. Directors should become aware of such opportunities and advertise them forcefully to their students, even if the students have already heard about them in their departments. This is an opportunity to secure research funding for honors students, especially as they plan and undertake their senior thesis. If the honors program resides in a research university, directors can also make a case for using some grant overhead or cost-recovery monies to support undergraduate research by their thesis students through an annual allocation. I persuaded the vice president of research to provide two $1,000 thesis fellowships, which, over a few years, we doubled to four, then eight. These were followed by two memorial thesis fellowships from the university library, perhaps because one of our Portz Scholar theses so impressed its dean.

Directors should consider other kinds of in-house collaborations. Our honors college was written into the first Ronald E. McNair Scholars program proposal as a host for its summer research program, part of the university's contribution to the program's support. Trio grants such as these rarely include an honors collaboration, but we have found it fruitful; it became part of our diversity mission, and we recruited McNair Scholars into honors and encouraged them to turn their McNair research projects into senior theses. No money came to us, but we benefited in other ways. Some major corporations endow or underwrite an institution's major undergraduate research program, as is the case, for example, of the University of Maryland's Gemstone project, which features interdisciplinary teams doing problem-based research over their four years. Directors may be able to make their honors program the centerpiece or at least an active participant in such a program.

Sometimes directors can leverage support for a project from multiple sources, internally and externally. Our inaugural art show was made possible by support from various funding sources: a Portz grant enabled us to purchase the permanent equipment (hanging system, pedestals, vitrines) that would allow us to mount the show each year, the dean of arts funded the catalog, the art school allowed us to share the spotlight with the annual BFA show, alumni volunteers (professional museum curators) served as judges, and a local art-supply business funded prizes. Directors must think creatively about putting together various pieces of funding to make a project happen.

Applying for grants can seem daunting, and directors should not waste time and energy on a long shot. If directors choose carefully and put in the necessary work, however, grant support from corporations, foundations, and government agencies is possible. I have placed it last in this first chapter because the other sections are more important and may be more immediately fruitful. Nevertheless, a baby step in the direction of grant-writing is a must as directors consider all the possible sources of additional funding for their program. If they feel hindered by inexperience, lack of time, and lack of help, they can pursue lessons on grant-writing through workshops, printed books and articles, and online resources. They can get advice from faculty and from the appropriate staff people in their development office and research grants office. The important step is to start.

This first chapter has been the longest because it covers so much basic material. Readers should now be convinced that they can do fundraising. Perhaps they have already taken some of the first steps toward securing new resources to enrich their students' learning experience and thus enhance their program's stability, attractiveness, and success. The next chapters will progress to new levels of ambition and sophistication in the areas already covered here.

CHAPTER 2:
FINDING THE PACE:
INCREASING THE MOMENTUM

Is it time for a pep talk again? If readers have taken the baby steps outlined in the first chapter, they should already be gaining some confidence from their increased knowledge of fundraising at their institution, from growing habits of stewardship and planning, and from the donations, no matter how small, that have started to flow into the program. Much remains to do, and directors can do it if they stand poised to invest more time and energy into stewardship, planning, training, writing persuasively, talking to donor prospects, and systematizing procedures. Rewards for these efforts await.

Stewardship 301:
Donor Activities

"Stewardship 101" stressed the importance of prompt and substantive thank-you letters to encourage and maintain contact with donors. Directors can also consider events and recognition as more ambitious ways to cement donor relationships.

Events

The events involving alumni mentioned in the preceding chapter clearly function not only to build the donor base but also to keep donors among them interested and inspired. Key events should be a part of stewardship activity. Directors can invite significant donors to major honors events, such as graduation recognitions, anniversaries, open houses, research forums, and performances. If their gifts have supported such events, directors can acknowledge them in the printed program and orally as patrons or angels, assuming that they have secured the donors' permission to do so. If a local business has underwritten the cost of food, location, or a guest speaker, directors should invite a representative to attend and to be introduced and thanked. For years a local independent bookstore had spiral-bound our publications free, saving us several thousand dollars, so we invited the owner and his family to our annual ceremony for seniors and acknowledged their support with a plaque. (I had also written a thank-you letter after each binding, with a copy to the foundation, and acknowledged the in-kind gift in the publications themselves.) Not all donors, especially those living at a considerable distance, will be able to attend such events, but they will appreciate having been invited. When donors do attend honors events, directors should welcome them personally and make introductions as appropriate, to staff and faculty members, university officials, or star students, including recipients of the donors' sponsorship or scholarship gift.

In addition to such formal honors events, directors should meet with current major donors from time to time by themselves, with a development officer, and/or, in the case of a special scholarship, with the student recipient(s). If directors are offering a meal or coffee, they should pay close attention to the donor's preference and convenience—a restaurant of his or her choice or a university dining room, meeting there or being picked up and transported, inviting others or not. Meeting a donor alone or with a development officer is appropriate for (a) becoming better acquainted, (b) further clarifying the donor's philanthropic interests, (c) ascertaining whether the donor is pleased with the way honors is using his or her gift, and (d) discussing the possibility of additional gifts—in other words for further cultivation. Including a student or students will give the student the opportunity to express gratitude personally and to give the donor a concrete sense of how his or her gift tangibly benefits students. Because this occasion is social rather than business, even if a development officer is present, it should reinforce the donor's good feelings about giving. Discussing explicitly any further gift in front of the student, however, would be inappropriate. Another especially useful occasion is a tour of the honors facility and one-on-one conversation in the director's office. Donors should see the program in operation, including ambient student activity or attending an honors class, and they are often flattered to be invited into the director's inner sanctum.

* Non-honors university events also cement donor relations, especially if they directly connect to the donor's interests or are major ceremonies to recognize donors. If a donor funds expenses of honors theatre seniors who are going out on auditions, the director could invite that donor to attend a play or an audition showcase, paying for the donor's ticket, of course. If the institution's student singers stage a Renaissance feast, the director could pay for a table to host several donors and their guests for a delightful evening. If the institution's development office invites major donors to the honors program to an annual scholarship dinner-dance, the director should plan to attend and sit with them. In some cases the director may be expected to invite them or even host a table. If any donors have given new endowments that year, they may receive a special distinction, and the director owes them the courtesy of hosting them and witnessing this recognition. One final suggestion from a mid-Atlantic

honors dean at a fundraising session at the NCHC national conference is to bring a donor to the NCHC conference. In that dean's experience, the donors he brought all returned more excited about honors in general and about his own honors college—and perhaps newly motivated to increase their donations.

All of these occasions allow directors to become better acquainted with their donors, to strengthen their personal relationships with them, and to talk about their program and their students. In all of the conversations that occur, directors must be disarmingly honest, sincere, enthusiastic, and straightforward. They must be good listeners. They will benefit from any information that could guide them in matching donor interest with their needs in any continuing contributions, but they should avoid the cynicism of thinking only in terms of such future gifts. They must establish genuine human relationships with their donors. They should honor the donors' philanthropy, their desire to do good.

Recognition

Honoring donors may take the form of public or private recognition. Even thank-you letters are a form of recognition. Directors can start informally with simple gifts, such as honors paraphernalia. If the program has a decent honors ballpoint pen, a magnet clip, a bookmark, or a letter opener, the director can with a humorous touch pull one out of a pocket at some point in the conversation, or such items can lie next to a place setting at a meal or in a folder of information. Our squeezable rubber brain, inscribed with our program name, never failed to evoke amusement. Directors might bring flowers when they go to pick up a donor for a meeting with a student or a music performance on campus. If they have a good photograph of the donor with students and perhaps themselves, they might offer a framed 8 x 10 version to commemorate the occasion. More pointedly, they could purchase a personal gift that matches the donor's interests and taste and then present it personally as a token of gratitude for support. If it also relates to the donor's gift, all the better; if the donor has established an endowment supporting students on a study abroad program in Spain, for example, a director might offer a small book on the Barcelona architect Antonio Gaudì.

At public events directors can honor a significant donor with an engraved plaque or clock, assuming that the donor agrees to a public acknowledgment. They can also recognize donors, excepting those who prefer anonymity, on the honors website, in newsletters and publications, and on wall plaques in the honors center. Institutional development offices often establish names or clubs for donors at certain levels of lifetime giving, essentially tiers of recognition, often referred to as giving clubs. They might be named for former presidents of the institution or for levels of involvement in a program. Our theatre school uses the following descending tiers: Producer's Circle, Director's Circle, Star's Circle, Actor's Circle, Ensemble, and Supporters. Directors can think of something similar that suits their program. They may find such identifiers hokey or crass, but they do give donors public recognition in monetary terms while providing a range of giving possibilities, even an incentive to strive to be included in the next tier upward. Such groupings also entail varying levels of privilege or perquisite, such as a special invitation to a private event in a trustee's home, a club dinner preceding a theatre performance, or seating at the president's or provost's table at a scholarship dinner. Directors can adapt such a method for their own donors. Some honors directors list donors according to such groupings on a signboard that can be regularly updated by computer and kept on public display. Others create a handsome plaque that lists donors to special fundraising projects, such as a facility renovation or a concentrated three-year campaign to create a study abroad endowment. For a donor who endows a scholarship with, say, one or two recipients each year, directors should create a permanent wall plaque showing the name of the scholarship and its donor and the recipients' names newly engraved each year.

In these forms of stewardship, directors should keep in mind the genuine emotional heart of the process: the generous intentions of donors and directors' heartfelt gratitude for their gifts. Inviting donors to events and finding ways to recognize them publicly are not games or manipulations, they are expressions of good will. Genial relations with donors may lead to further gifts, and this possibility may hover in directors' minds, but it should not be their primary motive.

Creating a Fundraising Plan

Each of the sections of Chapter 1 can be thought of as part of a director's fundraising plan. Some of them, such as thank-you letters and developing relationships with the administration and development office, work within an initial plan as startup tasks. Others, such as developing an alumni donor base, deciding on some modest fundraising projects, and exploring grant funding, may form part of an actual fundraising plan. These specific actions can lead to a fundraising goal. The point is that having a formal fundraising plan is critical to coordinating fundraising activities and directing them toward specific goals. It also communicates intelligent management and reassures donors that directors are thoughtful and strategic. Successful fundraising is intentional.

Ideally directors have developed the habit of strategic planning for their program—more likely, of course, if the program is on the larger side and they are full-time or nearly full-time honors administrators of whom such planning is expected. They may be required to align their strategic plan with that of the institution, but they may also be able to add specific honors goals that do not explicitly follow that larger plan. In the absence of institutional tradition or expectation, they will still find that creating an honors strategic plan is useful. Such a plan typically arises from discussions with staff and advisory bodies and ranges from a brief list of priorities for the next year or two to a chart with considerable detail. Directors may divide these priorities into short-term goals for the coming year and mid- and/or long-range goals for three years or five years out. Re-creating a strategic plan annually is useful in setting goals and in reporting progress in an annual report.

See Figure 1 for an example of the beginning of a well-organized chart for one-year goals that provides close guidance as a director carries it out. Each task implies a number of steps and collaborations; collaborators can be added to the column of parties responsible as long as a point person is clearly in charge. The last column can provide the actual results in boldface, with any explanatory notes. Directors may resist making too formal or detailed a plan like this because it seems too bureaucratic or it trammels them with too many promises or tasks. The most important element is producing realistic and measurable goals, which still stretch the program, and including in the plan the method for attaining them. Directors should not hesitate to be modest in choosing just a few major goals for focus; they do not need to take on everything at once. They should avoid listing standard maintenance tasks. They should choose goals that will advance the program through concentrated effort. They must also secure the agreement of those who will have some responsibility for carrying out the plan: agreement about the goals themselves, the methods, and their own area of responsibility.

This advice about strategic planning applies equally to an honors fundraising plan. Choosing a format consistent with the format of the honors strategic plan makes sense, whether it is a relatively informal list or a highly detailed chart. If directors are formulating a fundraising plan for the first time, they will probably include some infrastructure items, such as establishing a reliable alumni database. Even if all of these activities are yet to be undertaken, directors should also include a specific fundraising project, at least one item from their wish list, as an immediate start to securing donor support.

Figure 1. Example of the Beginning of a Well-Organized Chart for One-Year Strategic Goals

Objective	Tasks	Responsible person	Deadline	Measurable results
1. Develop a full-day orientation experience for incoming first-year students.	1.1. Coordinate scheduling to avoid conflict with other campus welcome activities.	Director Honeysuckle	10/2009	Specific date set
	1.2. Develop budget.	Director H. & Alice Azalea	11/2009	Completed
	1.3. Design activities on and off campus.	Alice & student council	3/2010	Completed
	1.4. Find faculty & student discussion leaders for summer-reading breakouts.	Alice	5/15/2010	Completed; # leaders & groups
	1.5. Secure transportation.	Alice	7/2010	Reserved
	1.6. Send letter to incoming students.	Director H.	7/20/2010	Sent
	1.7. Secure all materials and prizes & finalize schedule.	Alice	8/15/2010	Completed

One honors college in the Southeast listed its fundraising goals as follows:

- Increase alumni support.
- Retain corporate, organization, and foundation support.
- Increase friends and parents support.
- Increase the total number of gifts.
- Increase prospect and donor visits.
- Enhance donor communication.

These goals are broadly stated, but each can have specific targets and processes. For instance, increasing the total number of gifts could have a target increase of 5% or 10%, and the process for achieving it could be an alumni campaign.

A large honors program from the Midwest created its first fundraising plan to emphasize the following goals:

- Scholarships for incoming students.
- Study abroad scholarships for current students.
- Funds for research, creativity, and community engagement.
- Endowed honors research institute.
- State-of-the-art classroom, office, & meeting spaces.

Each goal was accompanied by an explanatory paragraph and a dollar target, with a five-year goal of $1 million. This well-thought-out plan also presented a list of recent accomplishments and a one-page general case statement for honors. Following the goals came (a) a list of five action steps, such as building a comprehensive list of alumni and conducting prospect research; (b) a list of 10 specific tactics, such as alumni events and stewardship letters; (c) a budget; (d) a timeline; and (e) a list of policies and procedures, such as annual progress reports.

As directors formulate a fundraising plan, they should consult others freely, listening carefully to the advice not only of their staff, faculty, and students but also of their administrative colleagues, alumni, advisory board, volunteers, and yes, even previous donors. They will also need to consult the development office and the person to whom they report. These administrators will need to give their blessing or authorization to honors goals, and they may eventually help achieve them.

See Figure 2 for a fundraising plan for three one-year goals modeled on the strategic plan format given earlier. As in the case of the strategic plan, directors may want to separate more immediate or one-year goals from long-range goals. The plan may include cost estimates for

Figure 2. A Sample Fundraising Plan for Three One-Year Goals

Objective	Tasks	Responsible person	Deadline	Measurable results
1. Develop an alumni scholarship endowment. (Strategic Plan Goal 2: Increase Student Scholarship Support)	1.1. Secure collaboration of honors alumni council.	Director Honeysuckle	10/2009	Council on board
	1.2. Find class leaders to help solicitation.	Dan Dandelion	11/2009	At least 7 leaders secured
	1.3. Seek lead gifts.	Director H.	2/15/2010	$10,000
	1.4. Do mass mailing of letter/case.	Diane Dahlia	4/20/2010	Completed
	1.5. Notify phone center of this priority, with script.	Diane	4/30/2010	Completed

Figure 2. A Sample Fundraising Plan for Three One-Year Goals (continued)

Objective	Tasks	Responsible person	Deadline	Measurable results
2. Increase study abroad scholarship fund. (Strategic Plan Goal 3: Increase Number of Students Studying Abroad)	2.1. Develop brochure of testimonials & photos from study abroad students.	Pearl Petunia	10/2009	Completed
	2.2. Notify phone center of this priority, with script.	Pearl	9/30/2009	Completed
	2.3. Ask current endowment donors to add $.	Director H.	12/31/2009	At least one donor increase
	2.4. Solicit area travel agencies.	Pearl	12/31/2009	$3,000
	2.5. Solicit international & well-traveled faculty.	Director H.	5/15/2010	$2,000

Figure 2. A Sample Fundraising Plan for Three One-Year Goals (continued)

Objective	Tasks	Responsible person	Deadline	Measurable results
3. Find business sponsor(s) for spring senior recognition dinner.

(Strategic Plan Goal 5: Improve Student Recognition) | 3.1. Develop brief case touting senior achievements, theses. | Dan Dandelion | 12/15/2009 | Completed |
	3.2. Develop list of likely donor prospects (e.g., banks, corporations, Chamber of Commerce).	Director H., Dan	12/15/2009	Completed
	3.3. Solicit for event support, thesis prize, graduation medallions.	Director H., Dan	3/1/2010	At least one sponsor secured
	3.4. Arrange for rep to attend dinner & be recognized.	Dan	3/15/2010	Done

brochures, mailings, travel, and any other specific expenses required for each particular project. The plan may also feature not just honors needs and priorities but also an emphasis on certain donor targets. Directors may wish to focus on increasing the number of donors, increasing the size of donations, getting previous donors to move to a higher level, securing major gifts, soliciting from faculty and staff, or using a challenge grant as an incentive to donors. They may use some or all of these approaches to achieve their project goal. Once they have completed the plan, they should make other key people aware of it, especially the person to whom they report and development staff members.

If their institution launches a capital campaign, directors may be asked to provide campaign goals for honors. (If they are not asked to do so, perhaps they should assert the right of honors to be a fundraising target in the campaign.) These goals will usually be major areas directors wish to be supported, ranging from a scholarship program or research support to a renovated facility. Directors will need to calculate monetary goals—whether $50,000 or $5 million—that are realistic given the larger picture of the institution's fundraising and the giving power of donor prospects for honors. These goals will doubtless reflect potential major gifts such as endowments, but a capital campaign also usually includes all gifts over a certain period of time. Thus directors will also have to estimate how much they expect to receive through the institution's annual honors contributions, which include any stray donations made independently of the campaign effort. With the help of a development officer, directors can determine a realistic goal.

See Figure 3 for an example of a one-sheet summary of campaign goals. The monetary goals directors set for several projects in the early stages of planning for a capital campaign may very well be reduced after administrators compare the proportions of dollar goals among all units and align honors totals with the overall size of the university campaign. As academic deans and athletic directors develop wish lists, they may produce an aggregate campaign goal four or five times what the campaign target should be, given the fundraising history of the institution. (Capital campaigns appear again in Chapter 3 in a section of their own.)

Whether directors are formulating an annual fundraising plan or a set of goals for a capital campaign, they may want to or be expected to attach to each project a brief statement of the need for this particular project and the benefits that will come from its success. (See Appendix C for an example.) This statement or brief paragraph will then be a useful starting point for writing the case statement—the persuasive document—to share with donor prospects and to draw on for various other communications.

Figure 3. Major Capital Campaign Goals for the Honors College ($x Million by 2014)

1. Senior Thesis Fellowship Endowments ($x00,000)

   Provide much-needed support for students undertaking the year-long senior thesis, a major educational priority for Honors and the University.

   Typical award: $1,000–$1,500 for the year; also desired: $3,000 summer stipends for summer science laboratory work.

2. Study Abroad Scholarship Endowments ($x00,000)

   Provide support for students undertaking study abroad, with its additional and rising expenses. A major educational priority for Honors and the University.

   Typical award: $1,500, but larger stipends needed.

3. Field Experience Awards ($x00,000)

   Provide support for experiential learning: conference attendance, research travel, field trips for Honors courses, service-learning projects, and community-based courses. A new strategic priority for Honors and the University.

   Typical award: $300–$1,000.

4. Annual Fund ($x00,000)

   Sustain academic excellence. Most contributions go to (a) the Honors Scholarship Endowment, which provides support for merit scholarships, and (b) the Dean's Discretionary Fund, which provides support for greatest needs: emergency student support, special events, equipment purchase, staff development travel.

At this point in directors' development as fundraisers and in their program's experience in securing private donations, and as part of their serious planning for the future, they may wish to assert the need for a development officer, assuming that they do not already have one. What goes into making the case? If the development model in place in the institution includes constituent development officers assigned to academic units, the precedent exists for directors to argue that honors should be added to the units so assisted. (If they report to a dean with a development officer, they should ensure that honors has a claim on that officer's attention.) They should check to see which other units are covered, which do not have development officers assigned, and what support the central office expects from the academic unit. Their case may be easier if honors has college status or if it has attained a level of maturity, stability, significant size, and alumni participation. They can argue that because of its special mission, honors deserves support of its own, even though its students also reside in the other academic units. They can use comparisons with rival honors programs that enjoy such assistance. They should show that honors is an attractive target for philanthropy. They should provide facts on the number of their alumni. They should explain that their job duties do not currently permit them to take on the tasks of fundraising alone. If another unit is unrepresented, such as the library, undergraduate research office, or a small college or school, they may suggest sharing a development officer as a start.

Directors may also have to express willingness to pay whatever the share of such a person's salary is normally expected of units, while arguing that with their much smaller size and budget than the degree-granting colleges it will be a hardship unless their superior can come up with some extra dollars. I had the painful experience of having to reallocate funds to cover part of a development officer's salary, but I was convinced by the usual investment argument: "It takes money to get money." One dean of a large honors college at a state university reported in an NCHC session that his investment of first half and then full salary for a dedicated development officer paid off in a huge increase in donations. If the institution does not have constituent development officers, directors should appeal for more attention and support from the central office. Without such assistance, their fundraising plan may have to be less ambitious.

As always, good planning ensures success. Fundraising activity will benefit from thoughtful preparation, selection of realistic projects and goals, and well-organized procedures.

Acquiring Some Formal Training

Many of the donor prospects directors meet in the fundraising process are likely to be more sophisticated about money matters than they are. In order to become more knowledgeable about fundraising, directors should at this point do some reading and consider attending workshops developed by professionals in development. They need to learn about planned giving, case statements, lead and pledge gifts, methods of solicitation, and above all, productive attitudes. Mastering the technical terms and processes is easy, and conversations with development office staff will guide directors at the outset. More complicated is sorting out how their own personality and values can aid rather than hinder their fundraising activity. From reading and workshops they will encounter personal anecdotes of lessons learned in the art of approaching donor prospects. These stories will be more or less instructive personally, depending on directors' own stage of development and their institutional context. At the very least such tales inspire hope and confidence that honors directors, too, can succeed at fundraising. Directors should remember, however, that their role in fundraising is not that of professional development officers but of academic program leaders whose expertise lies in academic values and knowledge of their program. They should weigh carefully the advice and examples; they should discuss any that seem inimical to their personal and academic values. They do not have to become different people, such as hand-pumping extroverts, to be successful at fundraising.

One starting point for reading, besides this handbook, is the library of materials in the institution's development office or books and articles available in the main library. A few select items are listed in the Annotated Bibliography in Appendix D. Directors may wish to start with some basic information about different aspects of fundraising, and they should focus on educational fundraising as the most relevant to their needs. A significant source of useful information is CASE, the Council for Advancement and Support of Education (http://www.case.org). This organization produces a series of general and specialized handbooks as well as periodicals and workshops. A recent catalog of new titles offers several useful works: Mal Warwick's *How to Write Successful Fundraising Letters*, Deborah Ward's *Writing Grant Proposals That Win*, and a CD called *Overcoming the Fear of Asking for a Major Gift*, a presentation by Marcy Heim. Workshops regularly appearing on CASE's calendar include "Introduction to Planned Giving," "Development for Deans," "Workshop for Newcomers in Development," "Persuasive Development Writing," and "Major Gift Solicitation: Making the Ask." Publications and workshops also cover stewardship, corporation and foundation support, and alumni relations. The magazine *Currents* offers useful trends, tips, and stories. For those CASE items that are too pricey for their budget, directors could collaborate with the development office or encourage that office to make the purchase for its own resource collection. (One example is Rachel Pollack's 12-page reprint of *Currents* articles titled "Fearless Fund Raising: A Guide for Faculty and Deans," available only in quantities of 25.) Other online resources abound, but I have chosen to be narrowly selective in the sites I have mentioned and listed in the bibliography.

Workshops and conferences offer special opportunities to learn more about fundraising beyond the printed word. Their advantage is the opportunity for direct engagement with fundraising professionals of wide and varied experience, both those who present sessions and those who attend. Directors will have ample opportunity to ask questions and to chat with others, including beginners like them. Such events may also feature small-group breakout discussions, self-examination, writing exercises, and even role-playing. In addition to the more extensive grant-writing (Chapter 1) and CASE workshops already mentioned, a number of regional organizations for fundraisers (e.g., chapters of the Association of Fundraising Professionals) offer one-day workshops that are easily accessible and less expensive. Directors should let their development office staff know that they are interested in attending and that they would be happy to accompany development staff to relevant workshops. Going with someone else eases the stress and gives directors someone to talk with about their workshop experience. As they strike out on their own, they may wish to take an honors staff person or faculty member with them. They should also determine if their own development office offers in-house training sessions on various topics, as in a number of large universities. If these are not available, directors could campaign to make them available to deans, chairs, and interested faculty.

How much formal study through reading and workshops directors need depends on their current comfort level and experience with fundraising. Most of the materials and resources available are aimed at professional development officers, but a few are designed for academic leaders. As directors learn more about professional fundraising, they will adapt what they learn to their own personality, purposes, habits of making relationships, and values as academics. As always, what they learn can help them grow in positive ways and help them carry out their primary, student-focused mission as honors leaders.

Developing More Ambitious Projects

As directors become more knowledgeable and confident and have found support for their modest projects, they can expand their ambition to larger goals. Some of these, such as the need for more space or a larger staff, may arise from the pressures of growing enrollment. Others may compensate for deficiencies or for previous lack of support from the institution. Some projects, such as an honors scholarship program or a library, might help the program fulfill NCHC's Basic Characteristics of a fully developed honors program or college. Some ideas may have lain dormant on a dream list, never making it to the wish list because they seemed like pipe dreams. Some may have dropped by the wayside because they depended on funding that never materialized from the upper administration. Now is the time to revive these ideas with a view of encouraging donors to share directors' passion for them. Now is the time to think about what could not only significantly improve the program but perhaps even transform it. An idea can be all the more powerful if it also serves as a model within the institution or community and has an impact beyond the borders of the honors program.

The larger or more complicated the project, the more thought and planning must go into it. Before investing excessive time and energy in so doing, directors should ascertain the feasibility of raising enough money to fund the project, especially if its success depends wholly on private contributions. For the more modest projects discussed in Chapter 1, they might succeed in securing funding through significant one-time gifts, including underwriting, grants, or aggregates of small gifts. Larger projects need major gifts, usually defined at a minimum as whatever the institution has determined is the threshold endowment level, ranging typically from $10,000 to $100,000. (Some major institutions define a higher level called "principal gifts" or "lead gifts," often at a minimum of $1 million.) Directors should ask themselves several questions. What makes them think that donors would be interested in their project? Have they already established a decent pool of donors interested in their program? Have they noticed a pattern in the funds these donors favor, the program aspects they like to support? Has the development office provided background research on giving capability and interest level among donor prospects who might favor a program representing academic excellence? Does honors currently have major donors who could be persuaded either to enlarge their support for their favorite project or to move to another interesting and worthy project?

Directors should bear in mind that donors are generally more interested in supporting people, above all students, than bricks-and-mortar projects. Of course, some donors are drawn to a renovation or building project if it will likely transform the program, raising it to a new level, and if their name can be placed on it. Donors are also not likely to contribute to the current expense budget. They want to make a difference beyond what the university currently pays for or should support. Directors cannot expect donors to become excited about endowing part of a staff member's salary or funding a computer update for clerical staff. Yet the goal of outfitting a student computer lab with desktops, printers, scanners, and multi-media merging equipment, or of adding to classrooms the smart boards or computer projectors that will enhance learning, might attract a donor's one-time gift because it directly serves students.

Another project that might draw some interest is a fund for guest speakers. Most of us remember the impact of an inspiring outside speaker visiting the campus. The speaker's charged rhetoric and fresh ideas may have led to our own significant intellectual development. Helpful to the argument in support of the project will be a plan to ask the speakers to visit a relevant honors class for a lively discussion or to engage in informal chats in the lounge with students. The more directors can enhance their students' experience of the speaker, weaving it into their overall honors learning experience, the more attractive the project will be to donors. Such speakers can still be found, especially in academia, for modest fees. With at least a $100,000 endowment, the honors program could afford two such speakers each year, one in fall and one in spring. Short of an endowment, directors might resort to local underwriters to jump-start the project with one-time funds. A full-scale artist/lecture series, where it is not competing with a similar university series, could become a far larger fundraising project. (See Chapter 3.)

Directors might also succeed in interesting donors in an endowed professorship, directorship, or deanship. (A more ambitious version of an endowed professorship and a building project will be mentioned in the next chapter.) Directors could seek a minimum endowment of $20,000, which would generate, at 5% annually, $1,000 that could be added to a highly sought faculty member's salary as a stipend for teaching a special-topics honors course. The faculty member would be honored as the Endowed Honors Fellow for that year. (Using the term "professor" or "professorship" should probably be reserved for the higher level of endowment that would fund a significant portion of the salary.) Depending on the donor's wishes, the donor's or a memorial name could be attached to the title (e.g., the Paula Pedagogue Endowed Honors Faculty Fellowship).

As the rapid calculation just mentioned suggests, directors should now become adept at quickly calculating in their heads how large an endowment is required to generate the desired annual income. They should know the minimum amount their institution currently requires for an endowment (e.g., $10,000, $25,000, or $50,000), how much annual interest (e.g., 4% or 5%) from its investment they can count on receiving in a spendable account separate from the principal, and how long (e.g., 12 months or 18 months) a new endowment must sit before it generates usable interest. These figures will influence their planning and their discussions with donor prospects. For example, if a donor endows a $5,000 scholarship with a gift of $100,000, he or she needs to know that a waiting period of a year will elapse before it can be activated. In other words, no student will benefit from the award in the year immediately following receipt of the gift. In such a case a director may persuade the donor, as I have done, to fund the first year up front with an additional one-time gift of $5,000. Then the donor sees the philanthropic purpose come to fruition sooner and receives the satisfaction of meeting the student and seeing the immediate impact on that student's life.

Scholarships, in fact, are one of the most attractive fundraising projects honors directors can offer. The honors fundraising plan might include the goal, for example, of securing one endowed, renewable recruiting scholarship per year in the first few years of new fundraising work in this area, depending on whether a development officer is available to help. As directors talk to donor prospects, they should ascertain the prospects' interest in directly supporting one of the best incoming students in this way. Perhaps directors would prefer the freedom to offer the scholarship to anyone they find worthy, but donors may be more willing to give if they can stipulate, for example, that the recipient intends to pursue a particular major. Donors might memorialize a parent with the scholarship, designating a type of recipient related to the parent's interests. Talking to donors not only about their interests but also about what they valued in their own college education can help directors make a connection to a current need or fundraising goal in their program.

Honors alumni probably completed a senior thesis and enjoyed enormous benefits from it. Now is the time to move beyond thesis sponsorships to substantive financial support for research. One approach is to announce to thesis sponsors, who have already proven to be interested in fostering the research and creativity of current students, the inauguration of a new general fund for research support and the search for gifts at various levels to establish a significant endowment that will permanently provide thesis support in the form of fellowships and travel funds. Directors can devise various tiers and give them names, starting perhaps at $500. They can supplement this approach by seeking fully endowed research fellowships from individual donors with that capacity. They can pursue local corporations with an interest in sponsoring students' research, asking these businesses either for one-time gifts or for endowments named for the firm. Securing significant lead gifts at the outset always encourages others to donate.

Recruiting scholarships and research fellowships may be particularly attractive to donors, but support for study abroad is another worthy fundraising project that may draw donor interest. Directors should find out which alumni benefited from study abroad themselves; they will know the sacrifices and benefits of such experiences. Those alumni who enjoyed the institution's study abroad program in the arts in Venice or in Spanish language in Costa Rica may now be motivated to support a student in that particular program. Directors can seek donor prospects who have become world travelers or who have worked in the Peace Corps or in multinational corporations abroad. They, too, will have the global perspective and cultural appreciation that might prompt a gift in support of students who wish to study abroad. If the honors student population is relatively provincial, the case can be even stronger and more appealing; the life-changing experience of a sojourn abroad may have a profound impact. Again the strategy may be three-pronged: to establish a fund from small donations, to find one-time gifts that will go directly to students, and to find endowment donors who may wish to specify a particular study abroad program or major or to place their name on the award.

In devising projects for support, the directors' imagination is their only limit. Often a project that arises from a felt need can achieve support in unexpected ways. One honors dean reports that many of his students desired to gain a primarily conversational ability in Arabic and Chinese for practical use in travel, but all of the university's language classes were comprehensive and deliberately paced. At the same time, he had met an honors parent, a father of three of his honors students, who was president of a local language training center. The dean made a telephone call. In partnership with honors, the center soon offered free intensive summer courses in the two languages; after three summers this in-kind gift was valued at $60,000. In this case a parent happy with his children's honors education held the solution to an honors need, and a watchful dean seized the opportunity.

At this point directors may still not have the fundraising success and pool of donor prospects to warrant the most ambitious, million-dollar projects discussed in the next chapter. Even though they are ready to seek endowment gifts with confidence, *it is still OKAY to think small*, to design projects that are feasible for this point in their history.

Writing Effective Case Statements

As honors directors develop large projects, they must establish the texts and scripts to persuade the donor prospects to whom they are writing and speaking. As they develop a project, their various in-house discussions and consultations will generate language about the concept of the project, the benefits to be gained from its success, and the attractions it might hold for donors. They will draw on this language in various ways as they speak with donor prospects extemporaneously, using facts and enthusiastic rhetoric at appropriate times as they gauge the individual donor's reactions and interests. They also must prepare a written description of the project and the argument for supporting it: this is called a *case statement* or the *case for support*. In its simplest form it may be a paragraph or two in a letter of solicitation in a mail campaign. More commonly, it is a separate document of one or two pages addressed to a specific donor prospect. For use with multiple prospects, it may take the form of a modest, printed, even color brochure. For very large projects, it may run longer and contain graphics such as drawings, photographs, and a project timeline and budget. As mentioned earlier, directors may also find it useful to draw up a general case statement for honors support as they formulate a fundraising plan. They can use some of its language to amplify individual project case statements.

The first principle of writing good case statements is to put oneself in the place of the audience, the donor prospect. This is really the basic principle of all persuasive writing, ranging from sermons to sales materials, from op-ed essays to campaign speeches. Here are two versions of a sample paragraph from a letter to alumni soliciting contributions to a research support fund, the first writer-centered and the second reader-centered:

> This year we have over 30 students bravely undertaking the senior thesis. They represent a wide variety of majors, ranging from art to zoology. They make great sacrifices, including reducing their part-time job hours, to fulfill this capstone requirement in our program. Some of them also encounter new expenses associated with their work. To date the university has not developed undergraduate research scholarships, so these students labor on with very little support. We have established a goal of increasing our current woefully small thesis support fund of about $2,700 to $20,000 over the next two years. Contributions of any size are welcome, but to reach our goal we are looking for some special angels who can with substantial gifts guarantee our success.

> This year 30 of our seniors are following in your footsteps by bravely undertaking a senior thesis. You doubtless remember vividly the toil and sacrifice you poured into your own thesis. You would also probably have welcomed the opportunity to apply for some financial support that would have encouraged you in your work—perhaps to make up for reduced part-time job income or to fund part of the expenses of presenting your work at a conference. With our fledgling thesis support fund, we are trying to

provide just that kind of encouragement for our talented students, and you can help! Your generous gift will enable us to expand this fund to our goal of $20,000 by 20__, and if your company matches your gift, you will move us along twice as fast!

The second-person pronoun in the second version emphasizes the facts by incorporating them into active, energetic sentences. By contrast, the first version sits back on its haunches. The second version also eliminates both the self-evident reference to the variety of majors and the negative images of the institution for its lack of support and for the "woefully small" existing honors fund. Again, donors will respond more favorably to the positive than to the negative, to quality than to need, and to future benefit than to current deficiency.

A longer and more formal case statement for major gifts may need to be vetted by the development office and by the director's superior. In some cases, the development staff will have some standard introductory language used on all case statements for major donors, perhaps something about the need for scholarships given rising costs, the historical context of the institution's success, or the importance of advancing stellar programs to the next level. Vetting a draft with an advisory board and even some donors can ensure that the document recognizes the perspective of the donor. It may also spark interest in these readers and lead to their donating to the cause.

These case statements may also contain references to the background of a specific donor prospect, connecting that person to the cause on the basis of a previous program relationship or known interest and helping him or her to envision the personal impact on the project of a significant donation. For alumni donors, the case can refer to what honors did for them when they were students. In some instances, for a prospect with whom some discussion has already occurred, the case statement may include specific dollar amounts either as a range or as a specific request. Again, this piece of persuasive writing should take a reader-oriented approach and should be dignified, straightforward, and concise. It should express both emotional and rational appeal, both compelling language or heartwarming depiction of benefits and the supporting facts that make the case credible. It should allude to the donor's values and to the values of the honors program. It should not convey all the arguments possible for the proposal but should be focused on the one or two that address the donor's interest. It should be memorable and urgent, encouraging immediate response. Busy and important readers appreciate grasping the project and the argument for supporting it quickly and easily without wading through excessive details or extravagant rhetoric.

The standard endowment case statement of a page or two has several parts. Their order may depend on previous conversations with the donor prospect. The *title* of the case is often the imagined name of the endowment: the name of the donor or person to be memorialized and the endowment's purpose. Either the opening or the closing provides *institutional context*, indicating educational mission regarding the function of the endowment, financial pressures on the institution, and/or specific strategic goals, such as support for undergraduate research, internationalization of the student body, or a capital campaign. The most important part of the case is the argument for the specific honors *purpose* of the desired endowment. This section requires vividly presenting the quality of honors students and the honors program that the gift will enhance, an evocation of the results of this new source of support, and some sense of the need for it for the honors program to accomplish its goals, its highest priorities. Perhaps leading up to the portrayal of the uses to which the endowment will be put will be some reference to the *donor's background*, ranging from an allusion to the donor's own educational experience, perhaps in honors, to a reminder of the donor's past support of honors or recent expressions of interest. The argument could connect the purpose of the proposed endowment to the donor's current career activity, suggesting, for example, the critical importance of study abroad in preparing students for the global marketplace in which the donor currently participates. Finally, the case usually includes a *climactic financial request*: a specific suggestion of a dollar figure, what it will provide for the students or program, and options for actually making the donation. Even when the request appears early and directly in a case statement, the details of giving options are typically saved for the end.

Here is a sample case statement for a thesis fellowship endowment, building on a discussion with an honors alum about one of his favorite professors:

The Simon Socrates Honors Thesis Fellowship

Thesis fellowships are powerful vehicles that encourage students to seize the challenge of doing sustained work of significant scope and substance. X, your past support directed to senior honors thesis students has recognized deserving students whose curiosity and ambition, in partnership with a knowledgeable professor, led them through a unique learning experience to realized success. Yet many students are unable to focus their time in this manner because they lack financial resources. **The Simon Socrates Honors Thesis Fellowship** would enable the Honors Program to provide students the financial incentive alleviating the need for part-time or full-time work as well as fulfill additional monetary requirements associated with some thesis projects.

The Senior Honors Thesis elevates the level of academic excellence to which all Honors students aspire. An endowed fund to increase this student opportunity will help sustain the Honors Program's dedication to rigorous thinking and ensure that commendable students receive financial backing. As you know, completing a thesis is rewarding in itself and can lead to continued research in the field. Of alumni recently surveyed who completed a thesis, over 31% had published all or part of the work related to it.

Honors Thesis Fellowships endowed at the level of $100,000, $250,000, or $350,000 provide support for many students of high academic achievement. You can thus offer much-needed encouragement through senior-year awards of $1,000 or $1,500 or, especially for science students, $3,500 awards for full-time summer research preceding the senior year, when such students would otherwise have to work full time for tuition money. Students working on a thesis raise the level of classroom discussion, spark enthusiasm among peers, and support fellow students in the learning process. Many of them present their work at conferences, win prizes, and find that the thesis aids admission to first-rate graduate and professional schools.

The Simon Socrates Honors Thesis Fellowship will provide support to a succession of talented students as well as a tribute to your favorite teacher who inspired you in ways you never thought possible. Honors advisors and teachers establish a special rapport with students that often lasts a lifetime. Your generosity in honor of Professor Socrates will not only help students financially but also educate them on the importance of giving back to their alma mater. Philanthropy is a learned trait. Alumni who give back serve as the best models for students now and to come.

Unrestricted endowments allow the greatest flexibility in awarding fellowships, thereby ensuring the usefulness of the endowment in perpetuity. X, you may choose, however, to designate that the Socrates Endowment be awarded preferably to students intending to complete a thesis in a particular program of study and/or to students demonstrating financial need. Endowments may be funded with transfers of cash or stock, and are payable over a period of up to five years.

The demands on institutions of higher education are remarkably different today from what they were even a decade ago. Declines in traditional sources of income, coupled with rapid changes in technology, have required most American universities to apply innovative strategies to maintain a high-quality educational experience while continuing to keep tuition affordable for most families. This is especially true in [state], where public support for higher education ranks below the national average and tuition rates are well above the average. At XX University, tuition for in-state students has risen from $3,740 in 199_ to $8,434 in 200_.

In order to remain affordable to families of modest means, the Honors Program must increase the level of endowed funds available for students. Endowments, because they provide a permanent financial base, are regarded as an important measure of the Program's long-term strength and stability. Endowment of **The Simon Socrates Honors Thesis Fellowship** is an integral component in meeting this important goal. X, we hope that you will join the Honors Program as a partner in this challenging and rewarding endeavor. Your support for the Honors Thesis Fellowship program will enrich the learning environment at XX State and provide for a succession of distinguished Honors graduates much like you who will continue to bestow the benefits of their talent and education on us all.

This case statement plunges right into the immediate purpose of the proposed endowment and opens out at the end to the institutional context after the dollar request. This organization makes sense when a director has already had enough discussion with the donor prospect to ascertain the person's area of interest and even an emotional motivation beyond philanthropy—in this case a desire to honor a former professor. The case shrewdly presents future benefits as an extension of proven current results showing the impact of the senior thesis. The case also expands the benefits beyond just the learning experience of the thesis for a particular student to that student's effect on the general intellectual level of the program and even to lessons about philanthropy. The monetary amounts are presumably a result of research into the prospect's level of giving power and interest, but the range of possibilities gives the person options. The periodic direct address to the donor, using the first name, may seem hokey, like the smooth tactic of a high-pressure salesperson, but it does engage the reader personally, making the document less abstract. Its use and its frequency are, of course a matter of judgment and style. Because case statements are often a collaboration with development professionals, directors should be alert to language that is culturally unacceptable to them and their donor prospect. They may compromise on some points but still rewrite to their taste whatever sounds alien, bureaucratic, or trite to the ear of an academic and of a donor. At the same time, many donor prospects work in the world of business, not academia, and may easily accept, even expect, an institutional fundraising language and tone.

Fuller case statements may be in order for the million-dollar goals discussed in Chapter 3, but they will follow a similar pattern. The donor prospect may need more substantive information and may be attracted by a few illustrations, such as an appendix with a budget and the architect's rendering of a new facility. Although much depends on the individual donor and how much previous discussion or cultivation has occurred, these case statements will usually not exceed five or six pages. Directors should still try to contain their entire message in these pages, rather than being tempted to supply, say, a CD with fuller data or visuals. Some donors, however, may prefer an electronic version of the document, or they may prefer that the case statement accompany an oral presentation, perhaps with PowerPoint. The written document then becomes a reminder that they can take with them.

Making Fundraising Processes Systematic

As honors directors engage in more of the activities related to fundraising, they will need to give some thought to efficiency of process. They should now make ongoing procedures as systematic as possible so that their time and energy can be focused on planning and on individual solicitation and stewardship.

Readers have already taken a first step by creating their own alumni records and by securing access to their institution's alumni database of honors graduates. As they have acquired good habits of stewardship, they may have developed a fairly standard thank-you letter, periodically updated, for small gifts to various honors funds in the foundation. They may now want to assign all fundraising clerical support to a single staff person if they have clerical staff, so that this point person will become thoroughly knowledgeable about their procedures, will receive duplicate notices of gifts as they come in, and will prepare the standard but personalized thank-you letters promptly for signature.

If directors have a development officer, or share a development officer, they may also be sharing clerical support for that officer, or they may have to provide such support from their own staff. If shared clerical support is located in the development office or another sharing academic unit, directors will have to go to extra lengths to ensure ready communication. In fact, such a shared support person may be charged to work largely for the development officer, scheduling appointments, handling his or her correspondence, and contacting the honors director when joint efforts are required. In that case, directors will still need in-house help in honors with their own personal stewardship correspondence, mass mailings, and meeting arrangements. Needless to say, they will charge any clerical support person they use with absolute discretion concerning the highly confidential and sensitive matters of fundraising and donor relations. One critical step in working with others is often overlooked: creating a written process description for all stewardship and fundraising procedures and sharing it with everyone engaged in them. Such a document should join others in the honors office's policies and procedures handbook.

Directors may delegate much to a secretary, including keeping paper and electronic files, but they may find it useful to maintain their own electronic files of correspondence, contact notes, and documents such as case statements. When they are ready to update a standard thank-you letter, they can easily go into their computer to revise the current one, relabel it, and email it to the secretary. They should create a separate electronic folder for each major donor so that their successive correspondence and contact notes will accumulate there and they can readily see what they discussed in previous communications. A paper folder will also be necessary to house paper communications from each donor along with copies of honors letters, emails, and other documents, including copies of formal endowment agreements. Directors can easily retrieve information about the donor's family, tastes, hobbies, even food allergies if they have included it in this central place.

Receiving and sending reports should also become systematic. Directors should ensure that their foundation office alerts them promptly to all new donations for honors, preferably at least weekly although some also do this daily or monthly. Usually such a uniform process is in place in the institution, but if gift reports are not readily and promptly forthcoming, if they are sent only to the directors' superior, or if honors has simply been neglected, directors should assert their need for the information. They may also be on an email list for monthly summary reports on gifts to the institution's annual fund, sometimes subdivided into telephone solicitation, direct mail, and other, and these reports should have a separate line for honors. Assuming that directors now have foundation endowment accounts, they should receive semiannual and annual reports on both the principal and the spending accounts. These reports should reflect various transactions: additional gifts, individual disbursements for scholarships or discretionary purposes, interest distributed, and service fees. Ideally, directors should also be able to call or email the foundation office at any time to ascertain current balances, with the caveat that some transactions they have authorized may not be reflected as promptly as they might wish. If they have a development officer working with them to cultivate donors, they should expect monthly reports from that officer about progress, goals, and new contacts to pursue. If the institution is engaged in a capital campaign, they can also expect periodic progress reports, including a line for honors. In all of these cases, they will see the importance of having honors fundraising affairs sorted out from the larger unit of which honors is a part. At any given moment they need to have ready access to the status of their foundation accounts and their fundraising results.

Directors' own reporting will also benefit from a systematic approach. In varying frequency they will want to share fundraising successes with staff, advisory bodies, and the person to whom they report. Given a detailed fundraising plan, they should provide progress reports on a regular basis. These will be at least annual, as part of their annual report, program assessment report, or personal performance evaluation. If the fundraising plan indicates deadlines for various activities, directors will need not only to monitor progress toward those deadlines but also to report the results when the deadlines have arrived to staff, advisory bodies, constituent development officer, and possibly their superior, depending on how closely that person wishes to follow their efforts. Some of this reporting shades into public relations insofar as directors wish to publicize successful fundraising results in aggregate to alumni and donors in general, and perhaps to their own students and faculty, or to prospective students and the public through the honors website.

Particularly important as directors approach one-on-one solicitations is to follow their development office's clearance procedures. They should build into their own planning a point early in a particular fundraising project when they check with development for approval to approach certain prospects. Every time they plan to approach a donor prospect they need to know not only that person's history of giving to the institution but also whether that person is currently being solicited by another unit. If they ask a prospect for a $5,000 study abroad scholarship while the School of Performing Arts has been cultivating that person for a $200,000 theatre renovation, the institution looks incompetent in the eyes of the donor. The institution also risks losing the larger donation if the donor can escape with the smaller one. Even for targeted mailings directors may need to provide a list of names to the development office to make sure that no one on the list is currently being cultivated by others. At the very least, the phone center might avoid calling any of those names during a two-month period following the honors mailing to avoid over-solicitation. Coordination is critical.

If directors have a development officer, they should establish a systematic process for working with that person. Whether or not this is a shared development officer, whether or not he or she has an office in the honors center, and whether or not directors receive email accounts of donor contacts from him or her, they should ideally expect to have monthly face-to-face meetings—all the more so if they are paying part or all of the development officer's salary. A development officer should come to each meeting with printed updates:

- a sheet showing the top ten donors being cultivated currently, with brief notes on progress with each,

- a second list of donors to be explored next,

- brief notes on imminent gifts, and

- requests for personal contact from the director, with or without the development officer, to advance a prospect to the next stage of interest.

Directors in turn should be prepared to

- account for their own fundraising activity in the preceding month,

- ask for background research and donation histories for certain prospects they may know personally, and

- plan donor visits, including travel to other cities, in accord with their schedule.

On a case-by-case basis, they should decide whether they or the development officer should take the lead with a particular prospect. The two should review together the progress of the honors fundraising plan. Because directors are preoccupied with running the honors program or college, they will need these regular meetings to keep them informed, maintain their momentum, and even nudge them to action.

Directors should bear in mind that their development officer may have been hired primarily to seek major gifts. Energetic and successful development officers may spend most of their time out of the office. Directors may need them to find help in the development office for other fundraising processes, such as a mass mailing or a foundation grant application. They may also seek assistance from a non-clerical staff member of their own for small fundraising projects. They may also consider their own time too valuable to spend on anything other than major gift solicitations. Many experienced fundraisers, whether professional development officers or academic leaders, believe that the financial returns for time invested in pursuing major gifts are far greater than those for time spent on broad projects directed to a large number of small donors. By considering the institutional context and the pool of donor prospects, the directors themselves can determine where they should focus their efforts.

If the institution maintains a phone center that hires students to make solicitation calls to alumni for the annual fund, directors should ensure that honors is on the list for targeted donations. They should encourage the head of the phone center to set aside certain times for students to call honors alumni and previous donors. Once honors has established a presence, directors can strengthen it by updating the information that callers use in their scripts. Here are some of the categories typical of such two- or three-page updates, whether on paper or electronic:

Honors College (or Program)

Dean (or Director)

Phone Number

Email

Fiscal Year

Date Last Updated

Current Enrollment

Faculty

Program News, Points of Pride

Major Events Forthcoming

Top Reasons for Support

Prominent Alumni

Major Programs

Projects Supported by Annual Giving

Directors can follow up on these updates with annual visits to the phone center to talk enthusiastically to the callers about honors.

Two other important activities should become habitual. Jotting down contact notes immediately after every conversation with a donor or donor prospect, whether in person or on the telephone, is critical. With time, forgetfulness sets in, and directors face the embarrassment at the next visit of not knowing something about the donor they should have remembered from the previous visit. Directors should also devise a reminder system for both cultivation and stewardship. If they have promised to send something to a donor prospect, they must follow through in the expected time. If they have offered to check back with the donor prospect after the three weeks suggested for considering a proposal, they must contact the donor promptly at the end of that period. Good stewards monitor the timing of contacts with major donors. Knowing readily when the last contact was made enables directors to remember when it is time to send a card, make a call, invite to an event, or send a newsletter. A monthly review of donor records may provide these helpful reminders.

The more directors can reduce some fundraising activities to routines, the more efficient they will become and the more attention they can pay both to the big picture and to the individual donors and donor prospects.

Making Cold Calls and Listening to Donors

Early on, honors directors acquire some experience with current donors, including major donors, with whom they have met face to face and established a personal relationship. If they have inherited these donors, they saw them initially as strangers, but the gifts were already established. Meeting them the first time was non-threatening, and an expression of gratitude was an easy conversation starter. Even if directors are prepared to ask such donors eventually for another gift or an increase in an endowment, their pre-established connection makes the encounter relatively comfortable.

What strikes fear into the heart of many of us is the anticipation of meeting a complete stranger whom we must endeavor to interest in funding our honors program. If the prospect is an alumnus of the program or at least of the institution, directors can assume some natural interest. If the prospect is an affluent businessperson in the institution's geographical area or an officer of a corporation that gives educational grants, the task is harder. In some cases the way may have been paved by a development officer who has steered the prospect to honors after previous conversations. If directors are actually accompanied by a development officer, much of the burden is also lifted. And of course, if they are natural extroverts, their personality and inclination will help them approach the meeting with confidence. Whether they find social relations stimulating or taxing, they should prepare well for the meeting and cultivate some useful attitudes about it.

Preparation

Some of this preparation is obvious. Has anyone else from the institution had contact with the donor prospect? Does the director have clearance from the development office to approach the person? What is the background of the donor prospect? Has the person donated to the institution before? What is the person's profession? Has the development office ascertained the prospect's giving power? Have any of the person's interests been identified—hobbies, philanthropic interests, family? Directors should also have full contact information, including cell phone number, so that they can contact the person readily if any glitch arises at the time of the meeting, such as a traffic snarl or a misunderstanding about time or place if the person is late.

Directors also need to clarify to themselves the purpose of the meeting. If it is a first meeting and the donor prospect lives close enough for repeat visits to be feasible, this may just be an opportunity to get acquainted by learning more about the person and telling the person something about honors. If directors are traveling to a city out of state, they must also take advantage of the meeting to move the conversation toward fundraising projects they have in mind. Either way, they should have in their heads a number of basic facts and points of pride about their program. They should refresh their memory about what sorts of questions prospective students, parents, and administrators frequently ask about their program: number of students, diversity, admission standards, graduation rate, advantages of honors education, placement of graduates, unique courses, and outstanding faculty. They should also go armed with good stories about individual student achievements: an interdisciplinary thesis, leadership excellence at the university, a major fellowship, or a conference presentation. In fact, they should prepare a folder of information about honors that will give the donor prospect an impressive overview. Its contents should not be overwhelming but could include a recruiting brochure, a fact sheet, an alumni newsletter, a publication or highlight sheet of student work, a list of current thesis topics or current special-topics courses, a few brief profiles of outstanding students (with photos), and perhaps a giveaway such as an honors-inscribed pen or notepad. If directors are emphasizing a specific fundraising priority, they should prepare the case statement for it and hand it to the prospect when introducing the topic. The folder then becomes something for the prospect to take home for later examination; directors should not waste meeting time and tax the prospect's attention and patience by going over each document in the folder.

As directors think about presenting their program, they should remember the donor's point of view. Yes, donors may be impressed by honors points of pride and by the proposed project, but they will want to know if the program is stable and well run, if it has institutional support, if it operates in agreement with the institution's policies and priorities. They will be confused and dismayed if the solicitation competes with a solicitation from another corner of the institution, suggesting that the director did not secure clearance to approach them. They will want assurance that the director is a leader who will make things happen, who will carry through with the proposed project and bring it to fruition. They will hope to infer from the director's personality, style, and language something about the director's integrity, values, and management style. Directors can meet some of these expectations through explicit reference, but others they will meet tacitly through their manner.

What attitudes will be fruitful as directors go into the meeting? First is a posture of respect for and deference to the donor prospect. Directors are seeking to establish common ground with this person, a partnership that will be gratifying to both. Their talk and their body language can be both energetic and enthusiastic without being overpowering. They should not talk too fast to get their point across. They should pause for interjected responses from the prospect. They should resist the professorial tendency to lecture! They should avoid any hint of arrogance in expressing their pride in their students and their program. They should never interrupt. They should convey confidence but also a willingness to learn and take suggestions.

A tangible sign of a deferential attitude is a courteous regard for the donor prospect's time. Directors should suit their schedule to that of the other person. Often such prospects are active people with their own priorities who are taking time from their busy schedule to see directors during a business day, or from valuable family time on the weekend. Directors may seek a meeting during lunch, coffee break, or cocktail hour as a natural time when donor prospects would expect to be away from immediate work pressures. Such periods offer more leisure for a comfortable conversation. Of course, directors will make clear that the prospect is their guest, that they will pay for the food. They should offer the prospect the choice of eating establishments. If they are choosing, they should select neither too fancy and expensive a restaurant nor a fast-food emporium; the former will raise questions about the program's fiscal prudence, and the latter could be taken as an insult. During work hours, however, directors may have only 15 minutes or half an hour of the prospect's time for what will have to be a highly efficient discussion in the prospect's office. If directors have agreed on a time slot, they should be sure to honor the closing time and take their leave when expected.

Second, directors should proceed with confidence; they should not *assume* sales resistance. If they are seeking a major gift, the donor prospect has the capacity to give it, and the prospect has agreed to meet to hear the proposal. Thus they can set out with some confidence. They should keep in mind that people with money expect to be asked for it. That is a realistic observation common among fundraisers. A more positive assumption is that people with money will have philanthropic interests, that they will wish to use some of their money not just to get a tax break but to give back, to do good in the world. The burden will still be on directors to secure the prospect's interest in their program, but they will not have to start from scratch by developing in the prospect a philanthropic impulse; they should assume that it already exists. (Of course, they should not ask the prospect what other causes he or she has supported.) They should also remember that they have in honors education a worthy cause for investment. Many people will enjoy being associated with the honors reputation for academic excellence, perhaps even more so because other segments of education sometimes elicit disappointment. Above all, directors should remember that the last 20 or so years in philanthropy have seen a shift away from the concept of charity to a concept of exchange or investment. Donors do not give just because honors needs the money and they want to feel good. They wish to see their gift used in a meaningful cause that is important to them and to society at large. They also tend to desire more engagement with the program and its students as a concomitant of their gift.

Having a flexible attitude is also desirable because the conversation may well take unpredictable turns. Although directors will have prepared key points, they should not give the impression that they are so wedded to a script that they cannot think on their feet. Despite anticipating the prospect's questions, especially tough questions, directors may still be called on to be improvisational, adapting flexibly as they listen carefully to the prospect. If they are well prepared with knowledge of their program and with good stories to tell, they should be able to shift gears readily.

All of these attitudes are enough to instill confidence in directors as they approach the meeting. Realistically, most meetings will not end with a gift in hand or even a promise. Persuading a prospect to make a major donation may take several meetings, even years, or may never succeed.

The common wisdom among fundraisers is that developing donor friends is a long-term process. Prospects will want to think about the proposal, consult family members, reassess philanthropic goals and interests, or seek more information, perhaps about the program or about pledges or deferred giving. Over the course of several contacts, perhaps some by telephone or email, directors may wish to invite the donor prospect to an honors event or to the honors facility for a visit. Despite the challenge of securing a donation in the end, they will need to develop some emotional immunity to disappointment, to abide delay patiently, to accept the "no, thank you" graciously, and to move on to other prospects.

The Meeting

Once a director has set up a meeting with a donor prospect, has dressed professionally, and has now arrived, greeted, shaken hands, and made introductions, what guidelines and advice govern such a meeting? The director has prepared well and has a sense of where the meeting should go. The director has intelligent questions to ask the prospect about his or her work and connection to the institution, or perhaps even to honors. The director has one or two particular fundraising goals in mind to emphasize as priorities. As in writing case statements, however, directors in this situation will need to think not so much in terms of themselves and what they want to say and hope to gain but more in terms of their audience and what that person's interests and motives might be. They must conduct a genuine conversation in which they are listening carefully to the other person. Their goal is to match the donor's interests to honors needs, and finding out what might spark the donor's interest may take a little time, often more than one meeting, for the discussion itself may further shape or change the donor's interest. Directors may have come prepared to emphasize one or two key initiatives, but as the conversation unfolds they may think of others that would better fit the donor's interests. In a half-hour meeting with a busy mid-career architecture alum in another city, I first unfolded our desire for thesis support or scholarship support, perhaps for a current architecture student, but before long what finally caught the person's interest was the idea of a study abroad scholarship that would enable a current architecture student to participate in the program's expensive semester in Europe. He knew from experience the value of sojourning abroad and felt connected personally to current students' need for support to make it possible.

Still, directors must balance galloping along any line of thought prompted by the donor prospect and making sure that they steer the talk to the point of the visit. Flexibility is critical, but so is assertiveness. Since directors have taken the initiative in asking for the meeting, they must take some responsibility for guiding the direction of the conversation. One danger is taking so much time for chit-chat—establishing a social relationship, finding out more about the donor prospect, and touting points of pride about honors—that directors do not have enough time to describe the fundraising project or answer questions. In a half-hour meeting they might allot 5–8 minutes for socializing chatter, another 5–8 minutes to introduce their folder of materials and describe a focus project or projects, and the remaining 14–20 minutes to answer the prospect's questions and to probe the prospect's interest in contributing something to their program and projects. The same proportions could apply to a one-hour luncheon meeting. Perhaps the most important and hardest lesson to remember is to allow ample time for the prospect's questions and responses, at any point and certainly in the last half of the meeting. It is easy to talk and talk and talk about our programs, but it is difficult to listen, which is our primary purpose if we are to match our needs to our donor's interests.

If directors are speaking with an honors alum, they might use the first or second meeting segment to elicit reminiscences about the program: What good memories does the person have of the honors experience? Who were his or her favorite professors and what courses were particularly memorable? What were the benefits of the thesis? Has the person accomplished something since graduation that speaks to the honors experience and that could be reported in the alumni newsletter? When I asked the reminiscence question of the architecture alum mentioned above, he volunteered that his semester abroad changed his life. Although this was not specifically an honors memory, I had no trouble in following this revelation by talking about some of our current third-year architecture students and the value as well as costliness of the study abroad program.

Whether the climax of the interview is a direct request for support, including a suggestion of dollar amount, depends on several things. As suggested earlier, if this session is the first meeting and the prospect is readily available for another meeting, directors may proceed gingerly, establishing a connection and getting some sense of whether the person is open to further discussion. Even if they have gone to considerable effort to visit a prospect in a distant city, they still may not be comfortable asking for a donation. Of course, if the prospect expresses decisively a lack of interest or a lack of interest at this time, they can offer some alternatives: other projects, smaller donations, pledges, or deferred giving. Or they may just bring the meeting to a cordial end with the hope of being able to return to the conversation at some future point. At another meeting with an alum, as I was approaching carefully my fundraising goal and raising the question of an endowment gift, the prospect suddenly announced that she and her husband were thinking of a million-dollar endowed professorship in her former department. Needless to say, I was delighted with the promise of such a gift to our institution, but any thought of a donation to honors was put on indefinite hold.

The situation will be quite different when development officers accompany directors on the interview. The two have different roles. The directors' job is focusing on their program—its quality, accomplishments, needs, and vision for the future—with enthusiastic details. This point is well made by my former provost, Paul Gaston, in an article in CASE *Currents* in September 2003 ("Top Dog: A Provost Offers Advice on Helping Chief Academic Officers Focus on Fund Raising"). Although he speaks mainly to fellow provosts, his message applies to all academic officers. He suggests that the academic officer's "inclination toward a reflective and discerning approach to individuals . . . might, in fact, convey precisely the authenticity and professional commitment some serious donors seek" (26). He argues that "the academic officer can be especially persuasive in describing" the needs of a program; the officer adds credibility to fundraising and helps ensure its "dignity and integrity" not just as "a pleading for funds" but as "the creation of mutual advantages for both the donor and the institution" (27).

The development officers' role is to take primary responsibility for moving toward and making the ask, and for explaining various donation methods. Still, directors should not be totally clueless about various financial arrangements that development officers might discuss; again some level of education about professional development matters is important. Directors' pre-established comfort level in working with development officers will ensure ease and flexibility about which person pursues or responds to particular lines of conversation with the donor as each meeting evolves. Occasionally donor prospects express a preference not to meet with development officers but with directors alone. Directors should honor such requests. Most development officers understand that the donor's wishes are what counts and that whoever can be most persuasive in securing a donation should be the contact person. If a donor has a particular complaint about a development officer, directors should take it seriously and promise to follow up and, if appropriate, correct the problem. They should show their respect for the development officer but not be defensive.

Good listening skills, cordiality, and enthusiasm about honors students and the honors program are critical to a successful meeting with a donor prospect, and the word "successful" need not necessarily mean a donation commitment at the time. The interview is successful if directors have represented their program well, made clear its strengths and needs, understood the prospect's perspective and interests, and established a genial relationship with future possibilities. Thus they should avoid any hard-sell tactics that will doubtless annoy the donor prospect and seem out of character with academic dignity and integrity. Of course they would be happy to receive a donation or pledge on the spot, but their major goal is to ascertain the person's interest in their program and in supporting the education of excellent students. They have achieved that goal even if the prospect is not interested, despite their winning charm and program attractions.

Although this section has focused on planned cold calls, directors should bear in mind that their conversations with potential donors often arise unexpectedly, perhaps as an offshoot of other activities or as a result of, pardon the expression, networking. Here is an instructive story from an honors director at a public university:

> I met my big endowment donors while co-chairing a committee to advance our library expansion/renovation effort. I was reluctant to accept the invitation to co-chair this library committee because I wanted to be working on raising money for the Honors Program. But while working on the library matter, I would always use the Honors Program students as examples of why the library needed to be expanded. These donors heard my examples and began to get interested in helping the Honors Program as well as the library. So, don't be too myopic in your vision of how to fundraise for your Honors Program. Donors could be lurking anywhere.

Paying attention to such tangential possibilities can be rewarding. If directors are generally bubbling with enthusiasm for their program and their students, and if they make a habit of establishing a sense of connection, some common element, with those whom they meet, they may be surprised at the benevolent interest that may flow back to them and their program.

Writing Grants

At the same time as honors directors are stepping up their efforts to learn about fundraising, to develop sophisticated stewardship and planning habits, and to approach individual donors, they should pursue potential grants from corporations and foundations. (Readers should return to the advice offered in Chapter 1 about securing money from organizations.)

The less help directors have and the more demanding their other tasks are, the more necessary is a priority choice among various fundraising efforts. If they have established one or more foundation accounts as described in Chapter 1, they may wish to concentrate their remaining time and effort at this point on securing major gifts through calling on donor prospects. They can defer grantsmanship until they have time or until it seems promising enough to warrant the extra effort. Seeing a number of prospects face to face may pay off more in the long run because directors are developing long-term relationships with already connected parties and can more readily add the force of their personality to their persuasive effort. Although a significant amount of that activity will be necessary to generate a single major gift, that gift may make as much difference as a grant, comes without the same kind of blind competition, generates a permanent payout, and lays sure groundwork for additional gifts in the future.

That said, now is a good time to become serious about grant applications if directors can manage this time-consuming process. Whether or not they have assigned someone on their staff—assuming that their program is of some size—to help coordinate fundraising, they may wish to assign a good writer on staff the tasks of ferreting out grant possibilities, consulting staff in the development or research office, and writing the first drafts of grant proposals. If their support staff is small, this responsibility will likely fall on directors. Certainly they are the ones to establish personal relationships with program officers at granting agencies. They should bear in mind, however, that such relationships may be prohibited by some funders, especially government agencies required to avoid bias, and some issue instructions not to contact them. Directors should determine whether the granting entity welcomes personal contact for questions and advice beyond published instructions.

Directors may have gained some experience by applying for small grants and finding local businesses or corporations to underwrite honors events or activities. They can look now for significant grants to support some of their larger fundraising projects. After they have found matches between what foundations or corporations might fund and the projects they have planned for honors, they should assess whether they can complete the proposal in the time available before any announced deadline. They should also consider how competitive the grant is: the more competitive, the more careful and complex the proposal. They should assess again whether a long shot is worth the effort, beyond giving them the practice at relationship-building and grant-writing. If the match is good and they are prepared to proceed with a proposal, they will also need to secure clearance from their development office. They need to know if some other unit on campus is applying to the same organization, and if so, which unit is to receive the green light or is already out in front. If all is approved, they can get started.

What follows is a hypothetical example of at least one successful scenario for a specific grant process with a modest dollar goal.

1. From her development office Honors Director Sondra Sage has learned of the Donald Doubledollar Foundation, located in Sin City, just 40 miles from her campus.

2. She finds a website for it and reads about its history, the kinds of projects it supports, the size of typical grants, and brief summaries of recent grants it has given. One of the foundation's preferences is educational projects that connect local schools to nearby colleges and universities. She also learns that awards are made on a rolling basis, with no fixed deadlines.

3. She has been trying to develop a community service project for which she needs funding: she hopes to recruit honors students as tutors for high school students who have failed state-mandated proficiency tests, in the hope that they will pass the next exam with this help. Her student advisory council has approved the idea, and an email survey of her students suggests that she will have no trouble finding recruits. Published exam passage rates and telephone discussions with principals in county high schools suggest the serious need for tutoring. The money—as much as $8,000—is needed to purchase review books in several subjects and pay for transportation for students between the high school and the campus. Space for one-on-one to one-on-three tutoring is available in the honors facility, an adjacent classroom building, and the library. Dr. Sage would like to run this program in five sessions every semester, leading up to the next exam, for two years. She will assess the results annually before continuing.

4. She secures clearance from the development office to approach the Doubledollar Foundation.

5. From the website she learns that the small staff of the Foundation is headed by David Doubledollar, the son of the original benefactor who established the Foundation. She notes down the contact information for David and other staff members.

6. She places a call to David, succeeds in getting through to him on a return call, and expresses her interest in applying for a grant. She sounds David out about her concept to see if it matches the Foundation's mission and to test his interest. She also asks for his advice about shaping the project. David sounds interested and invites Sondra to send him a one-page concept paper.

7. Sondra drafts the one-page concept paper that afternoon and runs it by her staff the next morning. It includes a paragraph describing the rationale or need for the project, including her discussions with principals and some compelling statistics; a paragraph describing how the project will work; and a brief budget table showing estimated cost of workbooks, transportation, and dollar equivalents for committed space and staff time. The amount totals $9,500, and she requests $8,200.

8. After modifying the draft and running it by a development or grants staff person over the next two days, Sondra drives to Sin City to deliver the paper at the Doubledollar office in person. She asks the receptionist if David happens to be in and available for a brief hello. She meets David, exchanges pleasantries, and hands over the concept paper, presented in an attractive folder with her business card. She assures David that she is eager for his advice on the project and offers both telephone and email as ways to contact her.

9. Two weeks later she receives an email from David, who suggests that she consider eliminating the estimated $2,000 transportation cost for the high school students either by sending her students to the schools or relying on their and their families' motivation to get them to her campus on their own. He recommends that Sondra write a full proposal, following the guidelines on the Foundation's website. Sondra thanks him warmly for his thoughtful suggestions and expresses enthusiasm about completing the proposal.

10. As she considers David's suggestions, she is doubtful that her honors tutors can all find transportation, even carpooling, to the schools. She is equally doubtful that she will achieve full attendance, especially over a five-week series of Saturday morning tutoring sessions, if students must find their own transportation to campus. She calls several principals in demographically different schools to ascertain their opinion on the issue. She learns that conducting the tutoring on school premises will be difficult, requiring paying a staff person to open the school and the rooms and to stay the duration, this cost ending up greater than the estimated transportation cost.

Nevertheless, she wishes to show David that she is taking his suggestion seriously and is incorporating it in some way. She also decides that David's strong encouragement makes the application process worth pursuing.

11. She begins planning the project in detail with her staff. Ruling out sending her students to the high schools, she decides that she could ask the high school students to find their own way to campus, at least for the first two semesters' trial run. In her proposal she will allow for the alternative possibility that after assessing this trial run, she may add transportation support to make the project successful. The Foundation grants are good for one year and offer the possibility of renewal for a second.

12. She consults the Doubledollar website for detailed instructions about submitting proposals for funding. She learns that the following elements, briefly, are required:

- Cover letter on letterhead from her

- One-page executive summary showing the title of the project, the amount requested, the purpose of the project, the Foundation's grant category the project fits, and contact information for the project coordinator

- Detailed description of the project, including background on the program, rationale or problem to be solved, amount requested, numbers of participants and schools projected, implementation plan and timeline, projected outcomes and method of assessment, other funding sources, plans for continuing the project beyond the grant (maximum 6 pages, 12-pt. standard font)

- One-page budget statement, showing specifically how grant funds will be allocated, including sources of cost estimates, and funds from other sources

- Support letters, especially from school officials involved

Aside from the cover letter, the proposal cannot exceed 10 pages. Submissions by email are unacceptable.

13. With her staff Sondra constructs a timeline for completing the proposal and assigns some tasks, such as securing accurate estimates on workbook cost, ensuring availability of tutoring space, and issuing a call to students for committed tutors. It is February, and she hopes to implement the program in the fall.

14. During the next few weeks she constructs the proposal, starting with the budget section because completing it will give her a detailed sense of how the project will unfold. She works out the project implementation plan, including how she will recruit both tutors and prospective students for the program, and sets the dates for the sessions in accordance with the subsequent exam dates. She writes the initial brief description of her program's mission, history, leadership, student service motivation, and successes, which establishes credibility. (This section may already be in her computer for repeated use.)

She fleshes out the description of the project, citing statistics and school leaders on the nature and scope of the problem, thus establishing a factual base for the problem and indicating principals' enthusiasm for finding help for their students. She demonstrates cost effectiveness by planning to re-use the tutorial books each semester rather than having students write in them or keep them. This plan also supports why she thinks that the project will be self-sustaining for a second and third year, unless new transportation costs are incurred or additional books must be ordered to accommodate a growing number of participants.

She shows that she has contacted the principals of all the high schools in the county as well as the county superintendent of schools, and she notes the number of schools that will cooperate in recruiting students to the program, with an estimate of how many students might participate out of the total who need it, sorted by school. She indicates the number of honors students already signed up to do the tutoring. She argues the advantages of highly intelligent tutors who are also close to the students' ages, and she describes the tutors' three-hour training program. She also notes the institution's in-kind support as dollar equivalents in the budget sheet: the campus facilities rental charge for an outside group and a percentage of salary for the project coordinator and for honors staff support. She also includes a cost for pencils and paper provided by her program to the students being tutored.

To demonstrate that she has thought through eventualities, she discusses how she will deal with high school students who show up sporadically instead of committing to the full five-week series. Her project assessment will be based on (a) the pass rate on the next exam following the tutoring, (b) the number of participants, and (c) their attendance. She will also assess the effectiveness of the study materials and tutors themselves through satisfaction surveys. One question will focus on transportation issues, and another on the motivation for attending or for missing sessions. Especially helpful in writing the proposal is the list of evaluation criteria on the Foundation's website. These serve as a checklist as she continues to review and refine the proposal. The obligation is to answer all the tough questions implied in these criteria as well as she can.

15. She has completed the draft proposal and now shares it for suggestions with an appropriate development or grants office staff member, her superior, her student advisory council, the high school administrators, and especially the two people from whom she plans to solicit letters of support: her most enthusiastic principal and the county education superintendent.

16. After making final revisions, she emails a copy of the proposal to her two key supporters, along with a draft of their endorsement letter that will save them time but that they can modify as they see fit, transfer to their own letterhead, and sign for inclusion in the grant proposal. She also asks for final advice from them about the proposal itself. She or her proposed project coordinator will pick up the letters when they are ready. Meanwhile, she is completing the executive summary and her cover letter.

17. After completing the final version of the proposal, including its support letters, she drives to Sin City and hand-delivers it in an attractive folder or envelope, with the three copies stapled as instructed, to the Doubledollar office. She chats once more with the receptionist, with whom she is now on friendly terms.

18. In the second week after submitting the proposal, she places a call to David to ask some questions about the review process. She could email him or ask for an appointment to talk to him in person, but she decides from what she knows of David that a phone call would be a happy medium between the informality of email and the too-formal time commitment of an appointment. On the phone David answers her questions about who is involved in reviewing proposals (he and two assistants), the review timetable (about six weeks), and when and how Sondra will be notified of the results (at the end of that period by formal letter).

19. Because she is new and unfamiliar to the Doubledollar Foundation, although it funded one other program at her institution several years earlier, she has decided earlier that an intermediary might be helpful in arguing her case. One of her advisory board members, she has discovered, knows David from serving with him on the board of

Helping Hands and Hearts, a social service agency in Sin City. Sondra has visited this board member with a copy of her proposal, explained it in person, and secured his willingness to speak to David, in a phone call in the third week after submission, to validate Sondra's credibility and that of her program (he's an alumnus) and the importance of the project to the high schools and thus to society at large.

20. At the end of six weeks, in May, Sondra receives the long-awaited letter informing her that her program will receive the requested $6,200 for purchase of review books for the program based on the number of estimated participants in the first year. Included are a contract form to sign and instructions about disbursement and about reporting the results at the end of the year.

21. She writes an immediate thank-you letter to David, accompanied by the signed form, and promises prompt updates on the project, including one after the first semester series. She notifies her advisory board member through a grateful thank-you letter to him. She also writes thank-you notes to others in the institution who offered advice on her drafts, and to the two leaders who wrote letters of support.

22. She shares the news with staff, the student advisory council, her superior, the high school principals involved, her institution's public relations office, and her students, faculty, and alumni as the occasion (e.g., a newsletter) warrants. She clarifies the new responsibilities of her selected project coordinator and secures his enthusiastic commitment. The first tasks will be to cement the commitment of the tutors for the series dates before they leave for the summer and to set up a project timetable.

23. It is now fall and her coordinator has purchased the books, high school students have been recruited, and the first tutoring series has produced a 65% pass rate among participants taking the next proficiency exam in the subject they had failed before. The number of participants has roughly matched the conservative advanced estimate, and the attendance rate has been good, if not perfect, for both tutors and students. Sondra sends a one-page letter to David summarizing this relative success and expressing the desire to increase the number of participants and the pass rate in the following semester. She also touts the success in other venues.

24. She performs the promised assessments at the end of the spring semester. The pass rate rose to 75% in spring, and the number of participants rose slightly. Paradoxically, attendance by the high

school students has been more sporadic, some complaining about the difficulty of securing transportation.

25. As required, she submits a final report on the grant project to David, following the instructions carefully and providing an appendix with the detailed assessment data. She makes a case for some additional funds for a second year to cover additional books and for transportation costs, specifically for renting two university vans to reach students in the most distant schools, which also happen to have the students with the lowest average socio-economic status.

26. She follows this report with an application for renewal based on these needs and on the success of the program after its first year. In this application she explains more clearly than she could the first time how the project, if its success continues, will become self-sustaining after the second year.

Throughout the application process, Sondra has increased her chances for success by

- meticulously matching her project to the funder's mission,
- following the grantor's suggestion for cost-effectiveness,
- carefully following instructions about the proposal,
- seeking advice from many others,
- establishing a personal relationship with the funder, and
- following the submission with savvy questions and the use of an advocate.

Her final report clinches her credibility and validates her project as worthy of modest continuing support for one more year.

Susan Golden offers some useful summary advice for the end of this discussion on grantsmanship. Here are her "Seven Winning Messages" for grant-writers to convey:

Message one: This project is important. It will make a difference.

Message two: We have thought through all the thorny planning issues; we may not have solved them all yet, but we have developed a strategy or a plan for handling each one.

Message three: I will deliver.

Message four: I will be easy to work with.

Message five: I really know what I am doing.

Message six: We are committed to moving ahead, whether or not the grant is awarded.

Message seven: The grant is crucial to the advancement of this
project. (104–107)

She points out that the last two, seemingly contradictory, require a careful balance between assuring the funder of the proposer's commitment
to the project and indicating that funding will allow it to happen sooner
or serve more people.

Grantsmanship is not for the faint of heart, and certainly directors
must be prepared for rejection. Grantsmanship can be a wonderful
learning experience for directors, and grants may allow them to bring
their vision to fruition.

Making Public Relations Systematic

Chapter 1 advised readers to send points of pride about their program
to the upper administration and to the development office on a regular
basis. Potential collaborators in fundraising need to be well informed
about the honors program quality. Hard work by directors and their staff
will keep honors in the institution's awareness and in the public eye.
Directors should systematize this aspect of their operation so that they
have many good stories in their heads at any time they need to share
them with donor prospects. They should also keep readily accessible lists
of such points of pride in their computer and in paper files. They may
also need to delegate to a staff member the responsibility of obtaining
the good stories, including testimonials, and keeping track of them.

If directors are required to complete an annual report or an assessment report, they should highlight their points of pride, ranging from
statistical generalities, such as an increase in admission or graduation
GPA, to individual anecdotes of student achievement (e.g., a physics student's summer research at Los Alamos or a journalism student's national
prize). This habit ensures that their immediate superior will be well
informed, but it also gives them an annual record that they can mine as
needed for points of pride to share with others and for longitudinal comparisons. They do not have to wait until the end of the year, however, to
share any good news from such assessment activities as course evaluations, exit surveys, and advising surveys. They can send such good news
at once to their immediate superior, the provost, the president, the development office, and the communications and marketing office, as well as
sharing it as the occasion arises with donors and donor prospects.

One of the more challenging tasks that directors face is to find out the
specific accomplishments of their students, faculty, and alumni. The
advising process will help if directors and advisors systematically request

this information from students at periodic advising sessions; in fact, they can include on advising forms a line for reporting any honors, awards, offices, and activities that they or advising staff can note down after asking students about them. They may also ask students to produce one-sheet profiles of themselves, with photos, that can be edited and used for a variety of purposes, including fundraising. Such profiles should include

- name,
- hometown,
- major(s) and minor(s),
- activities,
- community service,
- career goals,
- honors and awards,
- quotable testimonial about the honors experience, and
- other unique or interesting facts (e.g., adversity overcome, international travel).

Directors should also encourage students whose accomplishments are publicized in campus or public media to identify themselves as honors students.

Special accomplishments of honors faculty members are easier to uncover, with the help of internal institutional newsletters, conversations with department chairs, and personal communications with honors faculty members. Learning about alumni achievements is especially difficult and requires personal contacts in addition to the procedures established in alumni relations as described in Chapter 1. If directors know faculty colleagues whose children were in honors, these proud parents are a steady source of up-to-date news and contact information. Faculty thesis advisors also often hear from their graduates about their progress in advanced study or career. Update reply forms from the alumni newsletter and nominations for alumni awards will provide much good information. I overheard a faculty colleague telling someone about the twin daughters of one of his associates, about their success as faculty members in their own right. I happened to know that they were in honors years ago, so I secured his promise to email me their news and contact information. Directors should use every occasion to their advantage.

Once directors have acquired the ongoing habit of reaping these points of pride and having them ready at hand, they should consider all the possible means of disseminating them. Their enthusiasm for the accomplishments of their students will fuel their fundraising efforts. They should develop a collaborative relationship with the institution's communications and marketing office. They can suggest good honors spotlight stories for institutional publications, such as the internal newsletter and the alumni magazine. If an institutional marketing council includes academic representatives, directors should take a turn serving on it. For ready access, they should become acquainted with the specific staff members responsible for such areas as photography, publications, brochure design, media relations, and website. When an honors student receives an outstanding award, including a prestigious scholarship from the program, directors should secure a signed publicity waiver from the student, send a "hometowner" (a press release to the student's hometown newspaper), and add this item to the good stories they can share with donors and donor prospects. They can compose templates for such documents as the waiver and the press release to make their communications process more efficient. (See Appendix C for examples.) They should make a special effort to fine-tune the program website, making it attractive, up to date, comprehensive, and easy to navigate.

Attention to communicating the honors program's successes will pay off in directors' fundraising efforts.

Securing and Building Unrestricted Funds

The most attractive case for honors support for many donors is scholarship funding because that promises them the most direct benefit to students. But if directors have firmly established their program's reputation for quality as well as their own leadership integrity, they may find that many donors, especially alumni, will trust them to use donations for the purpose the directors deem most important. Some donors will also simply not wish to take the time to think about a specific purpose for their donation. Honors programs vary considerably in their needs, and major projects such as research support may be a top priority in fundraising and headline the strategic fundraising plan as well as budget requests to superiors. Directors should not underestimate, however, the importance of building an unrestricted or discretionary fund. It will comprise the most flexible of their donation monies, so they can certainly draw on it for whatever is their highest priority, their greatest need, at any given time. They will also find it a source of critical supplementary aid when small expenses arise that they could not otherwise afford. In fact, it can be a source of considerable comfort, all the more so if the honors budget is inadequate or the program has undergone budget cuts.

Let us assume that by now directors have established a dean's or director's discretionary fund account in their institution's foundation and that their appeals to alumni have succeeded in generating small donations that continue to flow in, sometimes as repeated annual gifts, to this fund as well as to a general honors scholarship fund. My experience with these modest donations has shown that scholarship donations outnumber discretionary donations two to one, but that the latter have still been sufficient to allow the discretionary fund to grow faster than expenditures from it. At this point directors should clearly advertise this fund, along with their general scholarship fund, as a preferred target for giving. They should make this preference known in alumni newsletters and on the honors website. They should reinforce it with their thank-you letters to donors to the fund. They may also make this fund the beneficiary of various projects, such as sales of paraphernalia or a used book sale, or of major events, such as an alumni reunion or an annual banquet, for which the ticket price could include a donation to the discretionary fund.

A technique for increasing the fund at a fast rate is attaching a request for some unrestricted funds as a rider to a request for a major endowment. Introducing such a note during the cultivation of a major gift usually happens only after that gift is fairly secure or has been committed. Depending on the donor's character and relationship to the director, such an additional request may or may not be feasible. But for some donors, it is worth a try. If directors have made the general case for honors convincing, the donor of even a memorial scholarship in psychology or of funding for a lobby renovation can understand the value of having discretionary funds to meet emergencies or to enrich students' learning experience.

The greatest advantage of a discretionary or unrestricted fund is what its name implies: freedom. With responsible judgment and staff consultation, directors can decide what to spend it on and when to spend it or save it. Because it exists at the mercy of incoming donations, they will take care not to deplete it all at once. If their institutional budget is adequate and they do not have many immediate claims on the discretionary fund, they should consider saving it, as I did, until it reaches the minimum level for an endowment, for conversion to an interest-bearing account, with a healthy amount left over to address current needs. An unrestricted endowment account, like all endowments, will generate discretionary funds in perpetuity, so it is a built-in hedge against future contingencies (except for the stock market!). The final step in securing unrestricted funds of some magnitude—through a major endowment of the program—will be discussed in Chapter 3.

CHAPTER 3:
BOLD STRIDES:
BECOMING A PRO!

Directors' dreams must not stop now that their multi-faceted and multi-layered efforts have created a steady stream of modest donations from a loyal base of supporters and their inauguration into cold calls and their search for endowment-level gifts have achieved some success. There are greater dreams ahead! My survey of honors administrators about their fundraising experience revealed program endowments ranging from $30,000 to $10.5 million, and a few much, much larger endowments have been reported in NCHC circles. Another NCHC survey resulted in a list of at least 26 honors programs or colleges that are named after major donors. One program can offer an orientation retreat every year because of a donor's endowment that covers its $20,000 cost. Another program found a donor who financed a major facility expansion. A third program secured an endowment that funds a large number of students to attend the annual NCHC conference. As directors dare to dream of transformative endowments, they can take several steps toward securing collaborative support and planning.

Making Honors Prominent in a Capital Campaign

Institutional capital campaigns do not occur often, but when they do, honors should be included in the planning discussions and be listed among the causes to be supported by the campaign. Directors may face several challenges in ensuring that this is the case. The campaign may not be planned democratically; the top administrators may dictate its goals and priorities. The campaign may focus on only a few institution-wide priorities, such as new buildings, endowed professorships or chairs, an undergraduate research fund, or a hefty recruiting scholarship project. In such cases, directors may not be able to place honors on the agenda, but they can prepare to do so for the next campaign through constant internal public relations efforts. If the program is small, or if it has not traditionally been perceived as important to the institution, the battle is again uphill. In the case of an honors college, the chances for a share of attention are probably better because of its enhanced status in the institution, as compared to program status. Although one honors college was not listed as a campaign priority by itself, its dean succeeded in having campaign leaders require all other academic units to address honors in their fundraising plans.

Capital campaigns are valuable to honors directors as well as to the institution because they intensify all fundraising and publicity efforts in the institution. They create donor excitement, even a bandwagon effect, and they may lead to an increase in ongoing donations afterwards. Special energy, often including a feasibility study by an outside consultant, is devoted to researching potential donors and to establishing target goals. The institution's detailed plan will help honors directors organize their own efforts. In such a plan the development office has usually set monetary goals at several levels, the number of donors required to reach those goals, and the number of prospects or asks needed to yield the actual donations. Below is an example of such a chart for a modest $100 million capital campaign.

Prospects	Gifts	Averaging	Equaling	Totaling
5	1	$10,000,000	$10,000,000	$ 10,000,000
10	2	5,000,000	10,000,000	20,000,000
20	4	3,000,000	12,000,000	32,000,000
50	10	1,000,000	10,000,000	42,000,000
60	12	750,000	9,000,000	51,000,000
125	25	500,000	12,500,000	63,500,000
250	50	250,000	12,500,000	76,000,000
500	100	100,000	10,000,000	86,000,000
750	150	50,000	7,500,000	93,500,000
1,000	200	25,000	5,000,000	98,500,000
Many	Many	<25,000	1,500,000	100,000,000

As mentioned earlier, a truism among development professionals is that as much as 90% of the target campaign goal may come from less than 10% of the donors. In a successful campaign at Cornell University in the 1990s, that 90% was funded by just 3.8% of the donors (Rhodes 7). In the chart above, 86% of the target is predicated on the proposed generosity of just 204 donors out of presumably more than 2,000 total donors, many of whom are simply renewing small gifts as part of the annual fund. Of course, such charts are abstractions compared to the actual flow of contributions that may or may not occur. The chart neatly assumes that five times as many donors must be contacted for every gift achieved. As campaign coordinators monitor progress, they will report data that may shift the expectations conveyed by the planning chart and that may require intensified fundraising efforts at particular levels.

As directors attune their honors fundraising to the campaign, they must assess where their own potential donors fit into a chart or plan like the one above, determining if they have any prospects capable of giving at the top levels. Historical trends in giving through the annual fund will allow them to predict how successful they will be in reaching their goal for the broad pyramid base of supporters. Research into honors prospects and patterns of past giving will help directors formulate their own version of the campaign chart and a realistic overall campaign target. Engagement with other units in the planning process will also identify the internal competition. In a capital campaign aiming at $100 million, for example, directors must determine what share of that total honors can raise. The goal directors choose and that is approved by the campaign organizers will also depend on what projects they have chosen to highlight in the campaign and the worthiness of these projects and their drawing power. (Appendix C includes a sample capital campaign case for support, highlighting three projects for a total of over $5 million.)

Directors must also consider how much help they will have in their effort and how much time they can take from the daily management of the honors program. The development office may provide additional staff and travel support. Directors may have someone on their staff already assigned to assist them in fundraising logistics, or they can reassign someone to take on this responsibility. If they have a development officer or shared development officer, that person must be energetic and optimistic about the higher level of activity demanded. Directors must commit themselves to the additional time and energy they must devote personally to meeting campaign goals. Once directors have asserted their program's visibility in a capital campaign, they must be ready to raise their own fundraising efforts to a new level.

As directors launch into the work, they should intensify all aspects of their fundraising, even if they focus greatest attention on major gifts that can make the greatest contribution to achieving their target dollar figure. Stewardship communications should reference the campaign and its special purposes. Concentrating on previous donors may generate surprising results. Another truism among fundraisers is that previous donors are the best prospects. Directors should rethink their methods of recognizing donors; they may need to move to a higher level or devise new and more gratifying strategies. They should enhance the honors website with special references to the campaign, certainly highlighting it on the alumni and donation pages. They should intensify alumni relations by starting an alumni council or engaging their current alumni council in the campaign. They should expend greater effort in finding alumni who have been out of touch, especially those who are mid-career and beyond, who have the greatest giving power. They should consider finding a donor who will create a matching fund as an incentive to other donors. If they have not established an advisory board specifically charged with helping to raise money for honors, they should now do so, and the board must have real work to do.

Directors do not want to be invisible in a comprehensive institutional capital campaign. This is an opportunity for their program to gain new ground, to gain new friends for their educational mission, and to carry the momentum gained into a higher level of private support after the campaign.

Establishing and Working with an Advisory Board

One helpful source of support not only for a capital campaign but also for directors' ongoing fundraising efforts is an advisory board, sometimes called an advisory council or board of visitors. Directors may already have established an alumni chapter or council comprising alums who wish to remain engaged with each other and with the program. An external advisory board is different in purpose, and one of its central functions is finding donors. (Other functions include promoting the program to the public and offering advice on how to prepare students for a changing world.) Directors may also expect its members to make significant personal donations themselves. Other units on campus will probably be ahead of honors in forming an advisory board, so directors should consult them as well as the development office for advice both on establishing their board and on maintaining its successful operation. Other honors programs and colleges have also established successful boards and are available for consultation. (See, e.g., Carnicom and Mathis, "Building an Honors Development Board.") Clearly directors should not think of creating an advisory board unless they have a clear idea of its function, have real work for its members to do, and can invest the time and energy to sustain it.

Directors should carefully select board members in consultation with their development officer or central office. The members may include honors alumni, but they can also include important business people and other leaders in the community or region, whether previously connected to the honors program or not. Usually, however, directors will have engaged their interest in honors, perhaps over several meetings, before taking the step of inviting them to join the board. The criteria for selecting effective board members are several. They should have a strong interest in supporting the program actively, rather than enjoying the honor without performing some work. They should be well connected in the world, so that through their work and other networks they can find new contacts for honors. They should be able to tell others enthusiastically about the program's quality and at some point introduce them to the director. Directors should approach these others as potential donors or as friends of honors who might supply honors with gifts in kind, guest appearances with students, or further contacts.

The board members should also have been screened by the development office as having significant giving capacity themselves. Some honors administrators stipulate to board candidates that a gift of a certain minimum amount, often at endowment level, is expected of membership. One dean of an honors college even requires board members to make a significant gift before locating, contacting, and soliciting others. Others approach the idea of a donation later, while first making members responsible for finding new contacts and for giving advice about the program's public relations. This latter task may seem minor, but board members, usually highly experienced in the business world, can offer an external critique of the honors publications and website that can be extremely valuable. Of course, the members must also commit themselves to meeting periodically, perhaps once or twice a year. Setting defined terms of office, such as three or five years, and staggering them give members a regular opportunity to decide whether they wish to continue or to drop off the board. Directors should contact members who miss three or so meetings in a row to ascertain whether they are still interested in serving.

How large should the advisory board be? That depends on the size of the program and the pool of potential candidates. A small honors program may do well to recruit a membership of five or six, a mid-sized program might need a board of 10–15, and a large college might need 20–25 members. The board of visitor bylaws of one mid-sized honors college prescribe a minimum of 12 and a maximum of 18. No matter how many members there are, not every meeting will likely have full attendance. The board should not meet more often than directors have work to accomplish, projects on which to consult board members for advice, and program updates to share with them. More than twice a year may tax the members' busy schedules. At least once a year is critical to keeping them engaged. Directors should tie the meeting when possible to a dinner with spouses afterwards and/or a campus event such as a play, concert, exhibit, athletic event, or, most usefully, an honors event. They should set meeting dates months in advance, and they should establish a listserve for the members for ready communication.

If directors have a development officer, that person will take some of the responsibility for planning meeting agendas as well as meeting with members individually to discuss their potential donation to the program and their contacts with other potential donors. Meetings should have printed agendas, some sort of student presentation, handouts of news about honors, and refreshments. Directors should observe the announced ending time religiously. They should do all in their power to help the members bond with each other in working for the common cause.

Some of the work of the advisory board can be done during the meetings. The development office, for example, can provide lists of donor prospects whom members might have known in their major or in honors during their college years. Members can review these lists during the meeting and note the names of those whom they know and rate the likelihood of their giving to honors. Between meetings they will then contact these acquaintances to talk about honors and ascertain their interest in meeting with the director and possibly finding a way to support the program. Another useful exercise during a meeting is having the members sit in a computer lab and browse the honors website, calling out where they find a problem in content, style, and navigability. Directors can take notes, discuss some reactions more thoroughly when they are contradictory, and then follow up with improvements to the website.

Advisory boards do not usually play a role in internal policy decisions concerning students and programs, but they may offer advice about the feasibility of various potential fundraising projects. Directors should keep board members as well informed as possible about the successes of their program and students so that members can help sell honors to potential donors and perhaps find an area that attracts their own philanthropic interest.

Creating Naming Opportunities

Although some donors may prefer to remain anonymous, often a naming opportunity provides a small emotional incentive in securing the gift in the first place. In calling on prospects, however, directors should not insult them by focusing heavily on the naming opportunity, as if vanity is their main motive. In the written case statement, personalized for a particular prospect, directors should name the endowment for the prospect so that he or she can envision the end result—say, the Vincent Intaglio Honors Scholarship in Art. In conversation, however, directors should save reference to naming until the gift seems forthcoming unless, of course, the prospect inquires about it sooner.

Directors should keep the focus on the good that the donation will do, on the prospect's presumed philanthropic interest. The naming may very well come as the last step. In fact, directors may wish to ask a prospect who has committed to a gift to take time to think about the naming, perhaps alternatively considering whether the gift could be a way to honor someone influential in the donor's life, such as a parent, or to memorialize someone deceased.

Because endowment naming is a pleasure for most donors, directors should have plentiful opportunities for naming available. From their successes with small endowments, they may already have scholarships named, according to donors' wishes, for donors themselves, relatives, or even a favorite professor. A major gift for scholarships, defined as the minimum for endowment status, usually earns naming rights. A Roman Gadabout Study Abroad Scholarship or the Thomas and Theresa Testtube Senior Thesis Fellowship will ensure annual awards to students in perpetuity. The donors have signed with directors and the development office an endowment agreement that stipulates the name, purpose, method of recipient selection, and distribution of the scholarship monies earned as interest on the endowment principal. Most donors do not claim a personal role in the selection of recipients, but they will enjoy directors' prompt notification and some description of the recipients' qualifications or plans connected to the purpose of the scholarship. For a competitive scholarship, directors may wish to ask the winning student if they can share his or her application essay with the donor. In all of their correspondence and publicity about the scholarship, directors should be sure to use its full, formal name accurately.

Large projects for funding students, such as a multi-million-dollar freshman recruiting scholarship program, will follow the same opportunity of naming as a single scholarship endowment. An endowment for a particular program, such as an orientation retreat, a professorship, or an annual two-week group sojourn abroad, can also easily be named for the donor. A one-time gift at a level comparable to that of a minimum endowment can also be recognized. Directors can honor the donor of all the equipment in the honors computer lab, for example, with a recognition plaque prominently displayed in the room. Naming the lab itself will doubtless require a larger gift associated with naming facilities.

Whether directors are creating a new facility, remodeling an existing one, or simply maintaining the current one, they can offer naming opportunities for it, both parts and the whole. They should ascertain, with the development office, what minimum donation is necessary for a naming privilege for a facility or part of a facility. For a new or renovated facility, fundraisers often determine this amount by dividing the construction cost by the square footage to come up with a price per square foot. Having determined the square footage of various parts of their space, such as a classroom or lounge, or for the whole facility, directors can calculate the minimum contribution needed. If the construction costs are paid by the university, the naming can still be granted for that minimum contribution even if it is designated for another purpose, such as faculty development. Naming may also recognize a significant lifetime giving record at or above the defined level. The naming then becomes a form of general donor recognition.

Naming is an opportunity for donors, but it is also a privilege. Directors may have a strong emotional impulse to name a room or a program for a beloved former director or dean or for a favorite honors professor who died prematurely in a plane crash. For such a purpose they could designate a scholarship they would otherwise award without an attached name as part of their recruiting program, but they should beware of giving away the naming privilege for a room or a project. They should reserve that privilege for a private donor whose contribution will add significantly to honors resources.

Developing Transformative Projects

Major naming opportunities are, of course, intimately connected with the development of suitably large projects. By now directors should be bravely contemplating some big ideas that will transform their program or college, ideas that may require funding at the million-dollar level.

Scholarships

One such project might be a scholarship program, as opposed to a single endowed scholarship. Such a program will not interest directors who believe, as some honors administrators do, that honors programs should not have their own scholarships lest students' motivation for joining honors be tainted by the attraction of, yes, filthy lucre. Such a program may also be out of bounds if the institution's policy dictates that scholarships should be dispensed centrally rather than being housed in an academic unit. If directors have had some success at securing modest endowed scholarships restricted to honors students, however, they may persuade the administration that they have the energy and momentum to earn many more private dollars for the institution and that they deserve to house them in honors accounts.

If directors have both the inclination and the green light to be entre-preneurial in establishing or expanding their scholarship program, they should use their planning process to decide on the form or forms their solicitation will take. A commitment to seek a mega-gift is an opportunity to rethink existing scholarship practices or devise new ones. Perhaps the greatest need is a large fund for recruiting high school students through renewable scholarships. If only about 5% of the interest an endowment principal generates in any year will be available to use, the scholarship fund will have to be huge to generate significant support for a fair num-ber of students.

Calculations about how much to ask a major donor prospect to con-sider depend on several variables. The size of the typical incoming class obviously determines to some extent the degree of support desired. Directors must also assess the extent to which scholarship help from hon-ors will be most wisely spent to maintain enrollment, to increase it, to enhance the enrollment of the highest-quality students, or to distribute the wealth more broadly to deserving students. A gift of several million dollars could provide competitive full-ride scholarships for the top stu-dents, support students across the board, or support those students in the lower credential tiers who have not qualified for scholarships previ-ously because honors has had so little to give. If every incoming student already receives a scholarship, a new endowment could increase it to make the program more competitive in recruitment. In calculating a tar-get request, guided by strategic and fundraising planning, directors may, for example, write a case statement that sets a goal of $10 million, which could generate $500,000 annually to (a) add 15 new full-ride scholar-ships at $20,000 each for $300,000, and (b) raise the current $2,000 scholarships of 200 students to $3,000, using the remaining $200,000. Directors should bear in mind that any scholarship tied to tuition or room and board will need to increase as those costs increase. They may need to set aside some endowment earnings to accommodate that future contingency.

Directors will also want to determine the relative roles of financial need and academic merit. How much financial need do their honors students have? Do they work long hours at part-time jobs and take out heavy loans, or is their socio-economic status or institutional scholarship support adequate without these methods of support? Is this the right time, perhaps because of rising costs or pressure from the institution or from politicians for access, to focus on need-based scholarships? The wis-est course during cultivation may be flexibility. The case statement may argue strongly for merit scholarships, for the need to be competitive to recruit the very best students and thus enhance the profile of the honors student body, but if the discussion with a donor prospect reveals a predilection for need-based aid, directors may want to accommodate that wish or suggest including in the agreement a preference for financial need among recipients. Rather than following a hard line either way, directors again must listen to their donor prospect. Securing any major scholarship gift will be a boon for their students.

Scholarship campaigns can also support other causes besides recruiting. A scholarship that starts only at the sophomore year, as in some honors programs, gives students a chance to prove themselves in the first year and apply competitively for an award that may or may not be renewable. One of the purposes of such a scholarship program is retention, rather than recruitment, of the best students. If the institution already offers renewable recruiting scholarships, such an honors scholarship will be welcome additional support for hard-working students.

A good case can also be made for supporting students who wish to study abroad. Many students cannot afford the extra expense or are daunted by such a sojourn if they are inexperienced. Even a modest one-time scholarship could enable more hard-pressed students to undertake such a life-changing learning experience, and it might just be the encouragement needed by the timid as well. As compared to a recruiting or retention scholarship program, a study abroad scholarship program can succeed with a more modest dollar target. Directors can calculate the amount needed depending on how many students currently study abroad, how many lack funds or are unwilling to go into further debt, and what target the honors strategic plan and fundraising plan have set for increasing the number of students studying abroad during the next one to three years. For example, the case statement might argue for a fund of one million dollars to generate new support money of $50,000 annually to award 25 students $2,000 each per semester or summer term of study abroad. The weight of the argument could rest on students' need for a global perspective and on a major honors and/or institutional initiative for internationalization of students' education.

Another attractive project mentioned earlier is support for research and creative projects, whether for the senior thesis, for independent study, for collaborative projects, or for summer tuition and stipend for preparatory research, especially in the sciences. Again, a single gift of even a half million dollars or a million dollars will generate significant scholarship support: $25,000 or $50,000 per year available by competitive application. It would support a strategic goal of increasing the thesis completion rate, which varies widely among honors programs but is seldom 100% and often far from it. Even if the institution already has an undergraduate research fund or the honors program has some money for research support, directors may still make a convincing case to the right donor. Potential donors for such a cause are not limited to affluent individuals. Businesses and industries often have a stake in developing research talent in undergraduates, and their foundations may be attracted to a well-planned research program such as the Undergraduate Research Opportunity Program (UROP) at the University of Michigan or the Gemstone Program at the University of Maryland. They may willingly support thesis research in specific areas compatible with the company's own work.

Directors may package a number of smaller projects under the heading of "experiential learning" to entice the right donor prospect. This broader category could include study abroad, National Student Exchange, service-learning projects, unpaid internships, conference attendance, and class field trips. It could even fund more imaginative projects, such as a student's proposal to spend the summer hiking the Appalachian Trail with the promise of a significant reflective journal or a substantial piece of creative writing. A fund generated by a large endowment could address all of these activities in proportion as needed. A donor prospect who has strong ideas about the limits of classroom or book learning and the need for practical learning experiences in the world may be pleased that an honors program, instead of being an elitist ivory tower, wishes to be one with that larger world, to have a porous boundary that encourages reciprocal relations with that community.

Helpful in any major scholarship campaign is an ongoing habit of inviting donors and donor prospects to student events, such as a scholarship recognition ceremony or a showcase for thesis research or study abroad. (See "Stewardship 301.") The stories students themselves tell about how much their scholarship support means to them may be the most powerful and persuasive arguments. These events should provide both formal presentations by students and opportunities for them to mingle informally with audience members. One honors director reports that after some years of using students for fundraising activities such as car washes and bake sales, she found that these events built community but did not raise serious money. Then she began inviting "four or five [students] to give presentations and to meet-and-greet at every Advisory Board meeting." She also held annual lunches for scholarship recipients and their donors. She found that "students were the best possible fundraisers. They were hip to how they could be helpful, and they were authentically appreciative of help to the program as well as to them personally" (personal communication). Many a donor's tears have flowed upon hearing earnest students speak glowingly of their academic experience, their difficulties overcome, and their gratitude.

Facilities

Less attractive than scholarships to many major donors, but still often successful, are improvements to honors spaces. Here again we are thinking about something transformative, not just knocking out a wall, refurbishing a student lounge, or adding an adjacent room to the honors facility. Multi-million-dollar donors are needed for major expansions such as adding a new wing, completely gutting and renovating another existing building, or constructing an entirely new building to house honors. As in the case of prospects who might be interested in funding a scholarship program, such donors are not easy to find, and honors directors will probably need the help of their development office research staff, major gifts coordinators, and even top administrators at the institution. Their own preparation must be even more thorough than for devising a scholarship program and its case statement.

A facilities project must again be part of honors strategic and fundraising plans, of course, and this implies heavy consultation and commitment from staff, students, and faculty. Of course, much more background work is necessary: directors should look at other honors facilities and talk to other honors administrators about what works well in honors spaces and how some of them achieved new facilities. They should conduct a student survey to determine priorities for the most important features in the new space. They should talk to their institution's architects, facilities planners, and space allocation committee about the feasibility of the project and its location. In fact, they will have to secure institutional approval for their plan before they can consider fundraising, unless a donor is already in the wings, and they may have to secure some institutional commitment for at least partial funding. In the case statement they should include an architect's rendering of a possible facility, with various elevations and a floor plan, as an enticing dream space that will move the honors program to a higher level and to higher visibility on campus. Perhaps such a project could be correlated to a move from program to college status.

Approaching key donor prospects for funding of a facility transformation will be subject to the same uncertainties as any cultivation. Directors may present their best case for the facility project but discover that the donor is really more interested in student support. They may tantalize with the attraction of a design captioned "The Milton M. Masonry Honors Center" but discover that the donor has little interest in a naming opportunity. Seldom will they appear before a high-powered prospect without a companion from the development office. In fact, the institution's president may be assigned as point person for the contact, making the case instead of the director, probably in more than one visit. That role flatters the donor prospect, parallels his or her status level, and shows institutional commitment to the building project. If the prospect does show interest, more detailed discussion is in order, including the timetable for construction, specific evidence of need for the facility, and possible scaled-up or scaled-down versions of the facility, depending on the donor's interest level and possible other funding. The eventual donor will receive regular updates from the director on the construction progress and become the guest of honor at the grand opening.

Artist/Lecture Series

Many institutions fund university-wide artist/lecture series featuring guests of considerable celebrity who will stimulate students and faculty and bring éclat to the institution and its local community through public presentations. Such guests may, for example, be elder statesmen, hot nonfiction authors, dance companies, actors, Nobel laureates, or journalists. Their fees are escalating, often ranging from $15,000 to $60,000 plus transportation, lodging, and meals. As a result of the rising cost, some institutions are curtailing or eliminating such speaker series, relying on individual academic units to bring in more modest guests to perform a similar function. Very large universities, however, can accommodate both a university-wide series and a more focused series, such as corporate CEOs and CFOs for a College of Business.

Whether or not the institution maintains a prestigious artist/lecture series or not, establishing an honors series may be desirable. Directors are performing a service to the institution if its own series is defunct, so in return they should garner some portion of institutional funding to encourage donors. If the institution maintains a series, directors can differentiate the honors series by conceiving of it as rotating annually among major disciplines or focused annually or biennially on a particular theme, such as biological ethics, cultural diversity, collaborative arts, or new cognitive paradigms in neuroscience. In fact, interdisciplinary topics and speakers would be especially suited to honors culture, as would speakers most abreast of innovative thinking in their fields. The argument for such a project gains weight if directors correlate a theme with a curricular theme for the year, or for a two-year period, thus integrating the classroom experience with the speaker series. They might, for example, find speakers relevant to their core required course sequence.

To undertake such a project, directors will again need to ask some critical preparatory questions:

- Do they have any experience already with guest speakers?
- Are they savvy about the world of professional agents?
- Do they have a staff member whom they can assign to run such an artist/lecture series, including negotiating contracts with the aid of the institutional counsel and mastering logistical details?
- How can they involve faculty and students in the process of selecting speakers and performing host responsibilities?
- Do they plan to have book signings, perhaps requiring collaboration with the bookstore?
- Will their faculty members welcome the opportunity to interrupt their tight semester schedules for classroom visits by the guests?
- Will students actually show up for the talks and performances?
- Will the events be widely publicized and open to the public, to get the most for the money and to lend importance to the series in the eyes of potential donors?
- Have directors consulted widely with people experienced with such series and with their own faculty and students to gauge in general which types of speakers and topics will attract a crowd?

When directors have answered such questions and are prepared realistically to undertake such a project, they are ready to seek a donor.

As in the case of endowing a significant scholarship program, a large endowment will be necessary to provide a stable, continuing artist/lecture series. Even a minimal series of, say, four speakers per year at a low average cost of $15,000 apiece, including expenses, would require an endowment of $1.2 million if the payout is 5%, more if the payout is less. If directors aspire to six annual speakers at a range of prices, they might need $2 million or more. If they wish to bring in a group of performers, even if not the full orchestra or opera company that I can remember appearing on my undergraduate campus, the costs will be even higher.

Whether the plan is modest or grand, directors should not neglect the possibility of leveraging some funds from other sources in the institution, such as deans, the provost's office, or the research office, listing them as co-sponsors. One honors program succeeded in securing financial assistance from college deans and the director of an interdisciplinary program to bring in guest lecturers as long as the events were open to the public. She reported that this proviso has "actually helped raise the profile of honors on campus and diminish perceptions of honors elitism!" (personal communication). Such support, even if token, from within the institution can persuade donor prospects that a speaker series is valued by the institution.

Finding the right donor for such a project will be a challenge. A prospect interested in the performing arts may not be particularly interested in intellectual talks. Directors must identify someone with breadth of vision who will have in mind the benefits not just to honors but also to the institution and to the community. Of the four high-level projects discussed in this section, this one transcends honors. The donor prospects to be cultivated may very well not be honors alumni. They may have been discovered by development staff, the provost, or the president. If they are affluent honors alumni, however, they may be attracted to the series as a way to enhance significantly the stature of honors in the institution and to make honors more visible in the eyes of the public. The case statement for the artist/lecture series should take into account all of the benefits mentioned here—to students, to the program, to the institution, to the community—in appealing to the donor prospect's philanthropic interests. The donor, once secured, will enjoy VIP seating available at each series event as the director's special guest.

Professorships

Although some honors programs and colleges have their own faculty or share joint appointments of faculty with disciplinary units, faculty members are still rarely assigned solely to honors. A change may be in the offing. In the preparatory discussion of NCHC's "Basic Characteristics of a Fully Developed Honors College," some honors deans made the case, without ultimate success, for honors-dedicated faculty as one of the characteristics, even if it be largely an aspirational goal at the time. A small trend is beginning as a few more honors programs have secured their own or shared faculty members.

Chapter 2 discussed the notion of an endowed professorship of a modest sort, perhaps called a faculty fellowship, with funding to provide a small additional stipend—say, one or two thousand dollars—to a stellar department faculty member teaching a special-topics or interdisciplinary honors course and enjoying the special named title for that semester or year. Now, however, readers are ready to seek an endowment that would fully fund a new hire or partially fund several joint appointments. An endowment of a little over a million dollars, for example, would allow directors to hire a new assistant professor in many fields in the humanities, social sciences, sciences, education, and the arts, assuming a starting salary of about $45,000 plus benefits. The growth of the principal, assuming a decent return, could accommodate future cost-of-living or merit pay increases. An alternative would be persuading the provost to fund the benefits cost.

Again directors need extensive planning, though not as extensive as for a facility. First they must decide whether having their own faculty member(s) is wise for their program. This decision requires much consultation with staff, students, and faculty, as well as with the person to whom directors report. In fact, if honors has never had its own faculty and directors have not had experience with supervisory authority over faculty, they may need special permission from the provost, assent from the deans, or even a vote from the faculty senate.

Many questions will arise during the process of obtaining permission and during the planning process:

- Does the honors curriculum justify having a faculty member?

- What will that person teach?

- Does the program need a specialist in a particular field in which there are a number of courses, such as a freshman writing course or a core curriculum seminar with a number of sections? Or does it need a generalist with strong experience in interdisciplinary studies and an ability to stimulate other faculty members to team-teach, develop new courses, and participate in faculty workshops?

- What will hiring a dedicated honors faculty member mean for the curriculum? Will it open new possibilities, say, for inaugurating special-topics courses? Will it allow honors to redesign its honors versions of departmental general education courses as a unique honors seminar series that will be more interdisciplinary and still fulfill general education requirements?

- Are directors committed to mentoring a junior faculty member, redefining the reward system (requirements for reappointment, promotion, tenure, and merit increases) to suit the honors role, and conducting the necessary performance reviews?

- How will directors characterize the relationship between their own faculty member and departmental honors faculty members who continue to serve honors students, especially if criteria for departmental honors faculty status already exist?

- Will directors need a special budget allocation to undertake a search once they have the endowed professorship in hand, and will the provost pay, or will directors be only too happy to fund the search process if they secure the desired endowment?

- Are endowed professorships already part of the provost's or institutional fundraising plan, and if so, will honors be competing with other units for donors, or will it benefit from a project already defined by the development office or upper administration?

Once directors have settled these and other questions, have secured permission to undertake a campaign for an endowed professorship, and have written an eloquent case statement, they will begin their search for a donor prospect, again with help from the development office and from their own substantial experience with honors donors.

If directors have already secured a minimal endowment gift for a faculty stipend, they may wish to return first to that donor to probe whether a significantly larger gift, providing an elevation of a fellow to a fully funded joint or full faculty member, might be forthcoming. Building on donors' previously committed interest when expanding a project in the same area is always wise. In fact, a renewed appeal to their generosity for a closely related project is in a sense a courtesy: directors are letting them in on the ground floor of a transformative campaign for a cause in which they have already invested significantly.

Directors may, however, need to find and approach new donor prospects, and in so doing, they will seek support not only from the development office but particularly from the provost. If they report to a dean, they should seek that person's help. If the provost or academic vice president is already campaigning for endowed faculty positions at various levels, directors should persuade that academic leader to include the honors position(s) as part of his or her approach to prospects. If the provost is not already so campaigning, directors should seek his or her help in making contacts and in leading or sharing the cultivation process. If the provost does no fundraising and the president prefers to be the point person, again directors should seek that person's aid in the cultivation. Much depends on how successful directors themselves have been in fundraising, how favorably the honors program is perceived by the upper administration, and how willing those top administrators are to see honors faculty as a worthy attraction in the competition for other institutional projects and for the institution's top donor prospects.

In the initial stages, directors might also wish to take one of their very best and most passionate faculty members with them on prospect visits. Such a person stands as an exemplar of all that is best about honors culture and pedagogy. In talking about his or her work with students in developing interdisciplinary courses and collaborative learning, the faculty member can convey an enthusiasm and deep caring about students' learning that may be more persuasive than anything directors can write in a case statement. Whether accompanied by a faculty member or not, directors should have in their heads their best stories about their faculty members' research expertise and work with students, as well as statistics from students' course evaluation forms. As in all persuasive communications, directors should not underestimate the importance of data. The case statement should include this support material as well, along with quoted testimonials from faculty and students. The donor prospect should readily perceive the crucial importance of recruiting the right kind of faculty members to teach honors students.

* * * * *

If a donor prospect declines interest in any one of these or other large-scale projects early on in the discussion, he or she may become interested in an alternative project in honors or in the institution. Directors will benefit from having other backup projects of significant scope, with case statements prepared, for just such a contingency. These alternatives should first be at the same level of funding, but directors can also easily fall back to a more modest project or to an enhancement of the donor's previous gift. Although I was refused on a $20-million ask, the donor subsequently added $25,000 to a previous endowment of half a million. The difference in amounts was considerable, but we were still delighted to preserve a solid relationship, increase the existing fund, and retain hope of additional future contributions.

At this point, a discussion of a rare occurrence might be wise: a donor's wish either to micromanage a project or to dictate a use of the gift that would violate honors or institutional policies. In the former case, few major donors, especially at the level presupposed by this chapter, will have the time or inclination to become involved in the design of a facility or the selection process for a professorship. At more modest levels, too, donors of endowed scholarships usually leave the selection of recipients to honors staff, even if they have placed some restriction, such as the student's major or financial need, on the award. Nonetheless, donors on occasion may want more say in the expenditure of their gift. Directors may persuade them otherwise by describing in some detail the in-house process and by reassuring them that directors will keep them fully informed of the timetable and of the ultimate result (e.g., information about scholarship recipients, statistics about the increased thesis completion or study abroad rate because of their gift, or photos of a construction process). Directors can also invite such donors to a scholarship celebration event, to the institution's facility in another country, to a research forum for thesis presentations, to a construction site walk-through, or to a grand opening. In other words, they can engage donors' desire for close involvement in other ways than in decision-making. In a rare case, however, with caution and careful judgment, directors may include the donors to an extent in that decision-making; donors might offer advice, indicate preferences for certain thesis projects or locations abroad to support, or offer professional expertise related to space layout and interior design of a proposed facility. A recent trend in general fundraising, and growing in higher education, is the donor-advised fund, in which the donor is engaged with, and is welcome to give advice on, the use of the donation. Legal control—and thus the ultimate say on the details of the use—is, however, reserved for the institution.

In the second case, even rarer, a multi-million-dollar donor may be presumptuous enough to desire a more proprietary interest in the honors program, dictating a new direction for it that would be unhealthy. Institutions have been known to reject significant gifts if they violate policy, tradition, or values. Sometimes much debate and considerable negotiation with the donor surround the decision to accept or reject. Honors directors, too, will need to consult seriously with their development office and top administrators if an imminent gift violates the academic integrity of their program. For example, a director could win an endowed professorship from a donor, but only on condition that the person hired teach a required honors interdisciplinary scientific inquiry course in such a way that it includes creationism alongside evolution. The director was looking for a faculty member who could work across disciplines in the sciences, but the plan was to create courses in global water resources and disease control, and the director certainly does not wish to accept a mandate to teach a belief that lies outside the entire discipline of science, let alone require such a course framework. Of course the director will clarify to the donor why such a purpose would be undesirable and restate the actual need based on collective planning and priority-setting. The director may present the difficulties of finding such a faculty candidate or suggest an altogether different project that might draw the donor's interest. Unfortunately, after conferring with superiors, the director may have to *just say no.*

A variation on this theme is others' solicitation of a gift without consulting honors directors, with the dismaying result that directors may not be able to say no. Here is a cautionary tale from a fellow honors dean:

> A recent, seven-figure gift was solicited by the director of development (and the president) without asking the Honors College what such a gift could best be used for; as a result, we are in a position of shifting priorities in order to accommodate the gift rather than the other way around. It's not a paradigm shift, but it is uncomfortable.

This example argues once more why directors must repeatedly impress the upper-level administration that they have an active fundraising plan tied to their strategic priorities. If top administrators are fully aware of the honors program's culture, needs, and priorities, they are less likely to act without consultation, and their solicitations, however well-intentioned and productive, are less likely to be misdirected.

Endowing the Honors Program or College!

Now for the ultimate step. Directors have developed an honors program or college of which they are justly proud. More than anything else it represents undergraduate academic excellence at their institution. Anyone associated with it enjoys something of its cachet for quality. Surely an affluent and philanthropic donor interested in higher education might be attracted to the noble mission of honors, be willing to support its further ambitions, and derive some gratification from having his or her name attached to it in perpetuity. The time has come to seek a donor who will endow the whole program or college.

Such an endowment likely needs to be much larger than a gift for a scholarship program, a building, or a professorship because it preempts any future opportunity to name the program as it grows and achieves even greater renown. The price required for such a gift has to be set carefully and in accord with institutional naming policies. Just as Chapter 1 stressed the importance of always having a wish list and an earlier section in this chapter noted the necessity of readily calculating the naming price for various facility spaces, so here directors must be prepared mentally with the minimum asking price for an endowed honors program or college in the context of their institution. This price may change as often as every other year, or it may be set for the duration of a particular capital campaign. The amount will reflect the size of the honors student body, the stability of honors traditions and operations, the status of the honors program at the institution, and the naming prices for other units. Although it is likely to be less than the endowment price for an academic college such as arts and sciences, engineering, or fine arts, the right to name the whole program should still never be sold cheaply. Unless the academic sector joins athletics in offering naming rights, such as for a stadium, to large corporations for a limited period of years, the honors program will not be renamed on a rotating basis to the highest bidder. Let us hope that we never see a Kibbles 'n Bits Honors College!

The case for endowing an honors program could be attached to a transformative elevation from program status to college status. The new status might appeal to a donor prospect if the case statement speaks of the national trend in this direction and the additional prestige and institutional commitment that will attend the change. The argument could also be attached to the construction of a new building, in which case the cost of construction could be included in what would then be a higher ask. The donor's name on the program or college sign on the new building effectively names the facility as well. If the university is already funding the facility, a collaborative in-house discussion will determine whether, for the right price, the facility naming can also be surrendered or whether the facility name should be reserved for a future donor prospect.

The paths to the right donor prospects will likely be varied. The president or development office staff may have scouted prospects who may not be honors alumni or anyone with whom directors have become acquainted in the course of their fundraising efforts. The donors themselves may have searched for the right project until finally directed to honors. Others may have cultivated them to the point of discovering that honors could be the right fit. On the other hand, directors themselves may have secured enough philanthropic interest and handsome contributions from a few donors who have much larger capability and whom directors could approach for this ultimate expansion of their giving. Perhaps a CEO on the honors advisory board is a friendly candidate. Not all honors donors or donor prospects may be people whose names directors would like to have on their program in perpetuity, but it would be wrong to refuse their gift unless they came by their filthy lucre illegally. Michael Corleone Mafioso, no thank you! Most serendipitous is the combination of a respected donor's means and motives with a director's well-established and genial relationship with that donor.

Directors must plan their approach to a donor prospect for this project by careful consultation, again, with the development office and top administrators. Although they may have tentatively mentioned the naming project to someone they already know, they are not likely to visit a donor prospect alone. For this momentous task their courage will be supported not only by their past fundraising experience but also by the professional expertise of others, probably a high-ranking development official or a top administrator. Some of the time they can rely on their partner to take the lead in the discussion. As always, their primary responsibility is to talk about the honors program: its quality, its history, its institutional support, its plans, its needs, its national standing, its worthiness of support at the highest level, its vision for the future.

As mentioned earlier, if directors' cultivation does not succeed, they may still come away with a smaller commitment or a gift that will expand a project in which the donor has already invested. If they come up empty-handed, they will surrender gracefully, depart cordially, and plan to inform this prospect periodically of their program news. If they succeed in securing the requested $10, $30, or $50 million endowment, they will have to work out many details. Lawyers may be involved, working with the development office. Perhaps the donor wishes to dedicate part of that gift to a specific project or two or to fund a totally new project that provides an unexpected opportunity for the program. The gift may come in pledged installments and the naming withheld until the pledge has been fulfilled. If the donor apportions the endowment among several major projects, such as a scholarship program, an interdisciplinary conference, and a professorship, directors may propose that some part of it also be dedicated to unrestricted, discretionary funds so that they have the flexibility to address future needs.

The ultimate triumph of an endowed program or college does not mean the end of the relationship with the donor. Of course directors will practice the highest level of stewardship following the gift—forever after, in fact—and the intensity of this stewardship will depend somewhat on the donor's preferences for being involved with the program. Of course directors will also think about how to revisit the donor after some time to broach the subject of additional gifts to support other projects. They should not just assume that after such a magnificent gift the donor will wish to close the relationship. As at all early levels of donation, a donor may make an initial gift as a trial, to see if it is used well and makes a difference, and to see if directors' stewardship is attentive and the program has further needs. A wealthy honors donor may conceivably become a continuing well of generosity.

CONCLUSION

Readers have been patient indeed as they have absorbed the prose of this handbook, so I will conclude with just a few basic principles. Directors should

- not be afraid to start small, yet concentrate significant effort on major donors and prospects;
- set a good example by becoming donors to their own honors program;
- show prompt gratitude and demonstrate how well each donor's gift is being used, for nothing encourages further giving better than good stewardship;
- cultivate relationships, not gifts;
- remember that previous donors are the best prospects;
- ask the right person for the right amount for the right project at the right time;
- solicit donors face-to-face, for this is the most critical and effective technique;
- remember that most donors do not give unless they are asked;
- treat everyone, even those they consider unlikely donors, with the highest respect, for surprises happen;
- remember that their attitude and flexibility count for much, for fundraising is an art more than a technique, and no advice or guideline can replace their own good sense, good judgment, good communication skills, and good character;
- learn from rejection and move on, preserving a cordial relationship for the future;
- go forth with enthusiasm and confidence.

APPENDIX A:
GLOSSARY

Annual Fund   Aggregate non-endowment giving, unsolicited or solicited ongoing through telephone or mail, sometimes to special groups such as faculty and staff.

Ask (n.)   (shudder) An explicit request for a donation, sometimes for a specific amount for a specific cause; also called the "solicitation."

Capital
Campaign   A major fundraising campaign by the whole institution, seeking to build its endowment and perhaps fund major projects (e.g., new construction). It has a *quiet phase*, a testing period before the campaign is officially announced and during which giving is significant enough to ensure success of the campaign goal (e.g., $50M, $400M); it can be either *comprehensive* or focused.

Case Statement   A carefully crafted written argument for giving for a specific purpose, usually custom-designed for a specific prospective donor or group of donors. Depending on the complexity of the project and the size of the request, this document may range from one or two pages to five-to-seven pages or longer. A general case statement makes a broad case for supporting the entity (e.g., an honors program).

Contact Notes   Notes written after every contact with a donor or prospective donor, recording the substance of the conversation, donor interests expressed, readiness of donor, questions to follow up on, and updated contact and personal information.

Constituent/Unit
Development
Officer   A professional fundraiser with ongoing responsibility for a specific area or areas of the institution, such as a department, college, library, honors program, or athletics; if available, a useful partner in crime.

Cultivate   No, this doesn't mean taking the hoe to the weeds in the carrot patch. Yet "cultivating our garden" (Candide's "cultiver notre jardin") metaphorically means taking care of business at home: getting needed financial support for our program by talking to potential donors and persuading them that they will be making an investment in quality. This term may offend, but it is common among fundraisers for the process of making purposeful fundraising contacts. The cultivation continuum moves from prospect discovery/identification through contact, solicitation, and commitment, to stewardship.

Development   A euphemism for fundraising. An institution's development office and its foundation are two separate but closely related entities—one raises money and the other receives, keeps, invests, and disburses it. Sometimes called "advancement," though that term is broader.

Endowment   A fund of determined minimal size that is invested by the institution's foundation in order to earn interest in perpetuity. The institution determines how much interest (e.g., 5%) can be paid out annually to the beneficiary (e.g., an honors program) in a spendable account, with the option of putting some of it back into the principal to help it grow.

Giving Clubs   Groups of donors classified hierarchically according to their lifetime giving and often publicized in a newsletter or display. Each club or tier has a name, and higher levels offer special privileges. Also called "recognition societies," they may offer lifetime membership or, say, a three-year term, requiring renewal of gifts for continuing membership.

Lead Gifts   Major initial gifts in a fundraising campaign, usually a capital campaign, whose size up front helps predict success in achieving the campaign's target amount.

Major Gifts   These are defined by the institution in monetary terms, often as the minimum amount (perhaps $10K, $25K, $50K) needed to create an interest-earning endowment.

Move (n. & v.)   An increase in interest, commitment, or giving level by a donor or prospective donor; as a verb, to persuade a donor or prospective donor to progress toward a commitment or to a higher level of giving.

Naming Opportunity	This is an available entity, physical (e.g., a center, room, or garden) or programmatic (e.g., an honors college, a scholarship, a study abroad program, or a speaker series) that for a specified level of giving can bear the donor's name or the name of his or her choice.
Payout	The percentage of interest earned by an endowment fund that is available to spend, often set at 4 to 5 percent, on a 5-year rolling basis.
Planned Giving	Also called "deferred giving," this term refers to bequests, charitable trusts, multi-year pledges, insurance policies, and other methods by which the donor postpones a gift but with promises expressed in official documents. Some financial instruments provide a living dividend to the donor and to the institution. Development offices often have specialists in these matters. Formerly referring only to bequests, the term has assumed a broader meaning.
Pledge	A commitment toward a gift total to be paid in installments (e.g., a pledge of $50K to be contributed in five annual installments of $10K). We hope that the donor does not renege! It is not legally binding, merely a statement of firm intention.
Prospect	A person or organization that has some likelihood of becoming a donor.
Prospect Identification	Research that discovers or qualifies donor prospects and is a necessary prerequisite to a fundraising campaign; often performed by a development office but aided by directors' own ransacking of their alumni files and their contacts with parents, faculty, community leaders, business people, plumbers, and others with cash.
Stewardship	The tender loving care exercised over funds donated and over donor relations, another term used in development offices: using the funds in accordance with the donors' wishes, reporting to donors how the funds benefited the program and its students, writing prompt thank-you letters, inviting donors to events, getting donors together with students and faculty, sending

donors points of pride and publications, generally keeping in touch with donors (telephone calls, greeting cards) and recognizing them as integral to the honors mission.

Underwriting Guaranteed partial or full support from a business or individual that will enable a project or event to occur.

APPENDIX B:
NCHC E-MAIL SURVEY, FALL 2007

1. Is your institution public or private, 2-year or 4-year?
   __ public 2-year
   __ public 4-year
   __ private 2-year
   __ private 4-year

2. Approximately how many honors students do your have?
   __ 0–200
   __ 201–600
   __ 601–1200
   __ 1201–2000
   __ 2001–

3. Are you a
   __ dean
   __ director
   __ other: _____

4. Is your honors position full-time or part-time?
   __ full-time
   __ part-time

5. Is fundraising part of your job description?
   __ yes
   __ no

6. Is fundraising increasingly an expectation placed on you by the upper administration?
   __ yes
   __ no

7. Approximately what percentage of your honors work time do you spend on all fundraising activities (e.g., correspondence, meetings, reports, visits, travel, social events) combined?
   _____%

8. Are you discouraged by your institution from engaging in fundraising for honors?
   __ yes
   __ no

9. Do you have any of the following help in fundraising?
   __ development officer fully dedicated to honors fundraising
   __ development officer shared with another unit
   __ central development office staff
   __ president, vice president, or dean
   __ other: _____
   __ none

10. If you have a fully dedicated or shared development officer, who pays the salary?

11. What is the aggregate market value of your program's endowment funds, if you have them?
    $_____
    __ We have none.
    __ I'd rather not say.

12. What is your comfort level (either thinking about or doing) with each of the following fundraising activities, on a scale of 1 to 5, 5 being the most comfortable?
    __ sending thank-you letters
    __ "talking up" your program
    __ working with a development officer
    __ working with your institution's central development office
    __ working with an advisory board
    __ working with an alumni council
    __ staying in touch with previous major donors
    __ holding fundraising receptions
    __ telephoning potential donors by yourself
    __ meeting potential donors by yourself
    __ meeting potential donors with a development officer
    __ involving honors faculty in fundraising
    __ involving honors students in meeting donors or potential donors
    __ soliciting donations from parents
    __ asking a potential donor for financial support
    __ asking a potential donor for a gift of a specific amount

13. What is the most important fundraising advice you would offer to other honors leaders?

14. Is there a book, article, or other resource (besides CASE) about fundraising that you would recommend to honors leaders?

15. In your view, what is the greatest barrier to honors fundraising success?

16. Are you willing to have me interview you by telephone about your
    fundraising experience?
    __ yes; tel. no.: _____
    __ no

17. The monograph will include brief anecdotes from honors
    fundraisers—success stories, effective practices, and cautionary
    tales—about any aspect of the fundraising process, preferably from
    honors academic leaders but also from honors development
    officers. If you would like to contribute such a story, type it in
    below, or think about it and send it to me in a separate email. These
    would be presented anonymously so that donor confidentiality
    would be preserved. You will have a chance to proof the final edited
    version before the manuscript is submitted.

    Here is my story:

APPENDIX C:
SAMPLE DOCUMENTS

1. Thank-You Letters (a.k.a. gift acknowledgments)

a. for an in-kind gift

November 10, 200_

Ms. Emily Enabler
Address
City, State, Zip

Dear Emily,

Thank you so much for your generous donation of a slightly used refrigerator (Montgomery Ward, 16.5 cu. ft., frostless) to the Honors College! We put it to immediate use.

The small refrigerator in our pantry has not been functioning well and is far too small to store food that we use for receptions and student meetings. Now we have placed your refrigerator in our new storage space for ready access when we need it for events. And since it's close to my office, that's where I keep my lunch pail, too!

Again, thanks for telling Sharon, our go-between, about your plan and for being willing to make us the beneficiaries. We're grateful.

Sincerely,

Grant

Grant Grateful, Director

cc: Gerry Greenback, University Foundation

[Note that it is neither necessary nor wise to state an estimated dollar value; the donor takes that responsibility when claiming the gift as a tax deduction. Also note the need to copy the foundation so that the gift can be recognized institutionally and an acknowledgment sent.]

b. for an alumni donation to a building fund

Congratulations on becoming an Honorary Hard Hat for the new Honors Program classroom addition by donating $1,000 to the building fund. Your generous gift will help bring to fruition this project to enhance our students' learning experience.

As you know from your own experience here, honors classes have been spread across the campus since the inception of the program. The new addition will provide four dedicated seminar rooms with state-of-the-art learning technology for our eager students and faculty. We envision a new sense of pride in honors pedagogy and an enhanced experience of the Honors House as an intellectual hub.

Your desire to help ensure this facility transformation is indeed gratifying. You will receive regular updates on the progress of the project, and you can also follow it on our website at http://www._____. We look forward to seeing you in the reserved section at our grand opening ceremony!

c. for an unexpected pledge

I have just received word of your pledge of $10,000 over the next five years for the Honors Program's General Fund. This is wonderful news! Your generous impulse to support our students and our educational work is heartwarming indeed.

We look forward to receiving your annual $2,000 installments toward this goal and to putting them to immediate use for the benefit of our students. You will receive a letter from me describing the specific uses of your gift, as well as ongoing copies of our semiannual newsletter. If you would prefer to let your gifts accumulate in order to convert the total into an endowment, perhaps for a named scholarship, I would be happy to explain how that might work.

Whether to discuss this option or just to become better acquainted and express my gratitude in person, I will be calling to arrange a meeting over lunch at a location of your choice. Thank you again for your thoughtful pledge to the Honors Program.

2. Thesis Sponsorship Solicitation and Reply Form

November 10, 200_

Mr. Anthony Alert
Address
City, State, Zip

Dear Anthony,

In the past your participation in our "adopt-a-thesis-student" project made a difference in our students' lives. Last year *all 57 thesis students were connected to thesis alumni or friends in this way.* Thank you once more for your generous donation!

We write to offer you the opportunity once again to support our thesis students. Because of your past interest, you have early choice from this year's list of students (enclosed). Just fill in the name(s) of the student(s) you wish to adopt on the enclosed reply form, and send it to us with your check for $150 per student in the enclosed prepaid envelope. Beyond the $100 of reimbursement for expenses to the student, the additional $50 will help build our Senior Thesis Fellowship Endowment; for the first time last year we were able to offer *two* $1,000 thesis fellowships from this new fund.

But wait (as the ad guys say)! This year we have another option. To provide more direct support up front to the student you have chosen, you can write that check for $500 for a scholarship stipend applied to the student's tuition and fees. With this greater level of support at the outset, the student may, for example, be able to reduce part-time work hours in order to concentrate more fully on the thesis. This approach may be a more satisfying way to support your student than to provide our normal $100 reimbursement for expenses at the end of the thesis process.

Four stories of current thesis students are particularly exciting:

- Matthew Milk, a Thesis Fellow, is undertaking *two* theses, one in each of his majors in art history and French.

- Jane Juice, a geology student, is building her thesis on the experience she gained and the sediment cores she collected from a research cruise in the Arctic Ocean.

- Karen Koffee is following her study abroad experience in Ecuador with a thesis in political science written in Spanish.

- Thomas Tea, a black studies and history double major, is researching the underground railroad in our area for a pamphlet that will be used by the county historical society.

As before, we will welcome any additional donation to the Senior Thesis Fellowship Endowment fund. Your gift will help us support additional thesis students as we continue to recruit more students to this ambitious work. If your company provides a matching gift, that will go to the fellowship endowment as well. Simply securing and completing matching gift paperwork can double—and sometimes triple—the impact of your gift to Honors.

We believe in all of these students, and we want to support them in their courageous undertaking. We are ever grateful for your help.

Sincerely,

Emeril

Emeril Eager, Dean

Yes! I am happy to support Honors thesis students again this year!

This year, I would like to support (4) (3) (2) (1) student(s) for $150 each. (*Please circle number of students.*)

Here is(are) the name(s) of the student(s) I have chosen to adopt:

                                                                    Amount

(1) _____ $_____

(2) _____ $_____

(3) _____ $_____

(4) _____ $_____

                                                       Total: $_____

To take advantage of your new option, I am eager to make a bigger difference by offering a $500 scholarship stipend directly to the following student:

_____

I am excited about the thesis fellowship project for these wonderful students who have followed in my footsteps, and I want to be among those contributing additionally to its endowment fund in the amount of

___ $1,000　___ $500　___ $250　___ Other _____.

Enclosed is my gift for:

$_____　Adopt-a-Thesis-Student Fund ($150/person)

$_____　Scholarship stipend @ $500

$_____　Additional Thesis Fellowship Endowment Donation

$_____　**Total Gift**

Name(s) as I wish it (them) to appear in acknowledgments:

_____

Payment Options

☐ My check, made payable to the *XX University Foundation*, is enclosed.

☐ Please charge my gift. (*Please complete information below.*)

    Type:　☐ VISA　☐ MasterCard

Card No. _____ Expiration date: ____/ _____

Account holder's name as it appears on the card:

_____

Signature: _____

3. Mail Reply Forms, with Options to Donate (modifiable for website use)

a. for alumni

INFORMATION UPDATE

Honors Alumni

The Honors Program would like to hear from you!

Please write so that we may let others know where you are and what you are doing.

Indicate also how you may be able to help us to continue the tradition of excellence you enjoyed when you were an honors student.

Name _____ (Maiden Name) _____

Address _____

City, State, Zip _____

Phone _____ Email _____

Degree & Year _____ Major _____

Other Degrees, Locations, & Years _____

Current Employer _____ Current Title _____

Spouse's Name _____ Alum? _____

News About You (e.g., awards, publications, promotions) _____

_____

_____

Check if you are interested in

___ Receiving Honors Alumni Council Information

___ Returning to meet with majors or to speak to students

___ Offering "shadowing" or an internship

___ Meeting other honors alumni in your area

___ Donating (see our website at www.____/gifts for a list of funds and projects that deserve your support, as well as a way to charge your gift online)
Check for $_____ enclosed.

b. for parents

HONORS PARENT SOCIETY FORM

Personal Information:

Name _____
Prefix   First   Middle Initial   Last

Address _____

_____

Home phone: _____ Cell phone: _____

Email: _____

Student's Name: _____

Please indicate your area(s) of interest:

___ EVENTS (such as Family Weekend, Homecoming, new student reception, Graduation Banquet, and cultural, education, and athletic programs)

___ CAREER NETWORKING (sharing professional and business expertise, internships, mentoring)

___ FUNDRAISING (assisting in securing financial support for student scholarships, study abroad opportunities, undergraduate research, internships, and program enhancement)

___ COMMUNICATION (newsletter, website, listserve, parent-to-parent advice)

___ LEADERSHIP (taking a leadership role in the development and organization of the Honors Parent Society)

___ DONATION (check for $___ enclosed)

___ Not interested in participating

___ OTHER _____

[Modified from an actual website; online the donation instruction can include a link to click on for instructions on mailing a gift or charging it directly online with the foundation.]

4. Student Publicity Waivers

HONORS PROGRAM
XX UNIVERSITY
ADDRESS, CITY, STATE, ZIP

HIGH SCHOOL STUDENT NEWS RELEASE FORM

Scholarship Received: _____

Name: _____
      (First)   (Middle Initial)   (Last)

Home Address: _____
      (Number)   (Street)

_____
(City)   (State)   (Zip)

Phone: _____

Parents' Names: _____
      (Mother)   (Father)

Parents' Home Address (If different from yours):

_____
(Number)   (Street)

_____
(City)   (State)   (Zip)

High School: _____

High School Activities/Honors: _____

_____

_____

College Major: _____Minor: _____

Career Plans: _____

Hometown Newspaper(s): _____

I, the undersigned, having read this document before signing it, do hereby release XX University and its employees to publish news releases and other promotional materials about the activities in which I have participated. I also agree to release such information to the donors of my scholarship. I hereby waive all rights to restrict this material.

_____
Student's Signature   Date

_____
Parent's Signature (if student is a minor)   Date

HONORS PROGRAM
XX UNIVERSITY
ADDRESS, CITY, STATE, ZIP

COLLEGE STUDENT NEWS RELEASE FORM

Recognition Received: _____

Name: _____
   (First)   (Middle Initial) (Last)

Local Address: _____
     (Number)   (Street)

(City)   (State)   (Zip)

Phone: _____

Parents' Names: _____
     (Mother)   (Father)

Parents' Home Address:

_____
     (Number)   (Street)

(City)   (State)   (Zip)

College Activities/Honors: _____

_____

_____

College Major: _____Minor: _____

Career Plans: _____

Hometown Newspaper(s): _____

I, the undersigned, having read this document before signing it, do hereby release XX University and its employees to publish news releases and other promotional materials about the activities in which I have participated and the honors I have received. If I have a donor-sponsored scholarship, I also agree to release such information to the donor. I hereby waive all rights to restrict this material.

_____
Student's Signature   Date

5. Press Release for a Hometown Newspaper

The Honors Program at Whitebeach College is pleased to announce that Sam Surfboard has been selected as the 2010 Wilma Wave Honors Scholar. He is the son of Jan and Ginny Surfboard of Sun City and will be joining the honors freshman class at Whitebeach College this fall.

The Wilma Wave Scholarship is a prestigious full-tuition scholarship established by its donor to support an incoming honors student majoring in geography. Dr. Wave was a long-time professor in that department who was revered by her students for her teaching excellence and her passion for her field.

This competitive award is based on an outstanding high school academic record and a compelling personal essay. Sam Surfboard is only the third recipient of the Wilma Wave Scholarship in the history of the Honors Program.

6. Case Statements

a. for endowing an honors college

XX UNIVERSITY
THE XXX HONORS COLLEGE

XX University seeks an unprecedented gift that will serve as a catalyst to advance our highly respected honors program. This fall, XX University will celebrate 25 years of excellence in honors education. The Honors College in many ways has helped the University to achieve its vision as a nationally competitive, student-centered research university serving [state] and the world.

A $24 million commitment over a period of years would endow The XXX Honors College and construct The XXX Honors Center. As the largest gift ever received in XX University's history, it will transform XX University, the Honors College, and generations of students and faculty. As a significant enhancement of high-quality teaching and learning, it will support the University's critical strategic goals for educational innovation for the diverse, global economy of the 21st century.

For The XXX Honors Center, $7,000,000:

Home to the XXX Honors College and approximately 900 students, the XXX Honors Center will feature seminar rooms, library, lounge, program and advising offices, and a guest apartment offering a new identity for the College at the heart of the intellectual life of the University. (See architect's rendering.)

For Student Support, $12,000,000:

- $10,000,000 in endowment to support a continuous total of 62 Endowed XXX Honors Fellows with $2,000 freshman renewable scholarships. These awards will complement the current scholarship program and recognize deserving students who are capable of great achievement but who have little or no other scholarship support (about 30% of our incoming class). Such a program will enable the Honors College to provide a renewable scholarship for every incoming freshman to alleviate the need for part-time work and allow greater focus on studies. Long a dream of the College, this goal suits our traditional values of providing opportunities for a broad pool of applicants, not just a small number of superstars, and will do more to transform the College than courting the latter.

- $700,000 in endowment to support 10 $3,500 XXX Summer Research Fellowships in support of senior thesis work. These awards are badly needed by science students requiring additional preparatory laboratory work but unable to sacrifice summer employment.

- $400,000 in endowment to support an annual $20,000 travel fund to support students presenting research at conferences, attending and presenting at the national and regional honors conferences, or participating in College-sponsored cultural excursions.

- $800,000 in endowment to enhance the current XXX Study Abroad Scholarships, raising each of the annual 20 awards from $500 to $2,000 and adding 5 new $2,000 awards.

- $100,000 in endowment to support 5 students @ $1,000 (or 10 @ $500) engaging in domestic off-campus programs such as the Chicago Internship Program and the National Student Exchange.

For Faculty, $5,000,000:

- $1,000,000 in endowment to recruit and support an Endowed XXX Honors Faculty Chair in Innovative Pedagogies. This faculty member will develop and teach new interdisciplinary, often team-taught, special-topics courses (currently in short supply in the College) that will serve as models for development of such courses across the university in an effort to transform general education.

- $1,500,000 in endowment to recruit and support an Endowed XXX Honors Faculty Chair or Associate Dean for Research Partnerships, charged to prepare greater numbers of students for the senior thesis and to advance undergraduate research across the university.

- $2,000,000 in endowment to strengthen curriculum through support to departments for the release of distinguished faculty to teach honors courses. Current part-time faculty funds are inadequate to support courses in danger of being dropped by departments or to secure all-honors versions of currently mixed classes, in keeping with the recommendation of our external program review. This fund will also provide part-time salary to outstanding emeriti and other faculty recruited to teach in honors.

- $500,000 in endowment to provide $500 stipends to 50 faculty directors of senior theses. Their work often continues through the summer and may require special materials or equipment.

b. for a capital campaign (minus color photos)
THE HONORS COLLEGE
MAKING A DIFFERENCE TO OUR FUTURE

The Honors College is the magnet that attracts the best and brightest students to XXU. These are students who are recruited by every top-ranked school in the U.S. and in whom substantial educational resources are often invested because they hold the greatest promise for significant, even world-changing achievements. Their presence at XXU raises the bar in every classroom and affects the overall quality of the educational experience on our campus. Every year, Honors College students earn national and international recognition for their academic excellence. In 2002, Honors student —— became XXU's first Rhodes Scholar, underscoring the importance of Honors education in preparing outstanding leaders who will make a difference.

Developing Great Young Minds and Leaders

The Honors College is designed to provide a challenging and exciting academic experience to talented students who have demonstrated an ability to achieve scholarly excellence. Housed in a facility that inspires creative and disciplined thinking, our program combines the intimacy of a small liberal arts college with the intellectual stimulation of a large research university. Honors students receive an education that prepares them to enter the best graduate and professional schools, as well as distinguished careers in business and public service. They are individuals who will become the leaders who will shape our future.

Honors classes are small, and course work crosses traditional disciplinary boundaries to encourage critical thinking. Beyond the classroom, special guest lectures and presentations, study abroad programs, and volunteer service activities expand the horizons of honors students and contribute to the formation of citizen-leaders. A true community of scholars is being created in the honors residence hall. Honors students also receive special scholarships, incentives that may not only affect their decision to study at XXU but also enable them to pursue their studies with greater financial security. These special academic opportunities that constitute the honors program contribute to our success in attracting the best young scholars to XXU and in providing them with a truly exceptional academic experience.

How You Can Help

Maintaining a strong honors program at XXU depends on supporting critical needs that are not totally met by state funding. Our desire is to complete our residential facilities for our living/learning community and to establish endowments to support our students. Endowments generate annual income that would address these needs without depleting the initial capital investment. A named endowment fund may be established with a minimum commitment of $25,000 in any of the project areas listed below.

Needs

The following outlines the funding priorities for the Honors College. These needs will be addressed through private philanthropy and include: the *Honors Living and Learning Center,* the *President's Scholars Program,* and the *Pre-Medical Scholarships for Students Serving Underserved Communities* for a total of $5.64 million.

1. Honors Living-Learning Center in X Hall

Proposed Gifts
$300,000 to name Learning Center
$300,000 to name and endow program

The Honors College is pleased to announce the Fall 2007 opening of its "Living-Learning Center" in the newly constructed X residence hall. In addition to the state-of-the-art apartment-style facilities, X Hall will feature a 12-month calendar of campus life activities and programs designed specifically with the honors student in mind. X Hall will house 460 beds and an office shared by the Honors College and XXU's Housing and Residence Life. A gift with matching state funds would enable the Honors College to construct four multi-media classrooms and a small library in X Hall. A grant of $40,000 has already been secured for the equipment and technology needs of two classrooms. Moreover, additional gifts will make it possible to support a faculty-in-residence program and a comprehensive residence life program in X Hall.

2. President's Scholars Program

Proposed Endowment
Goal of $1.02 million

The importance of study abroad to the formation of scholar-leaders cannot be overstated. ——, XXU's first Rhodes Scholar, stated that his experience abroad was the single most important factor in his successful bid for the Rhodes award. Mr. —— competed in a field of students from Ivy League schools such as Harvard, Dartmouth, and Princeton, whose students regularly receive financial assistance to expand their horizons in becoming global citizens. The President's Scholars Program for Study Abroad provides a $5,000 scholarship to honors students on a competitive basis to participate in the special XXU honors program at YY University. The funding requested would provide an additional 12 scholarships to worthy Honors students.

3. Endowed Scholarships for Honors Pre-Med Students

Proposed Endowment
Goal of $4.02 million

Historically, honors colleges across the nation have served as "pipelines" for medical schools. Because honors colleges attract the best and brightest students, medical schools seek to attract honors student applicants for training in medicine. With the announcement of XXU's new medical school, the Honors College will become the university's pipeline for pre-med students intent on pursing a medical degree (M.D.) or advanced degrees in the biomedical sciences. Honors students pursuing advanced degrees in the natural sciences would also be eligible for this scholarship. Moreover, the Honors College seeks to recruit students who intend to practice medicine in central [state] or underserved regions of the state. This endowed scholarship fund would provide annual support of $5,000 to each student for a total of 40 students (four cohort groups of ten students starting as freshmen).

Total Honors College Capital Campaign: $5.64 million

7. Contact notes

Fred Firmgrasp—Contact Notes

Visit by Gary Gladhander; Topsy Turvy restaurant in Dallas, TX, lunch on Saturday, January 21, 200_.

- Remembers fondly Honors courses in English, philosophy, thesis on Russian nationalism

- After KSU graduation, to TX for various jobs, then graduate work in international relations (fall 1967), served four years in Air Force, then joined reserves; translation experience led to xxx job, now in Dallas with xxx Corporation; work is high-security government projects

- Still has relatives locally and returns once a year; married with two sons, now college graduates

- Typically splits annual donations between Honors and Political Science, feels he doesn't know enough about Honors to choose a particular program to support; I asked him to look over the materials I left with him and went over the main scholarship needs & campaign targets; he tends to respond to annual mail or phone solicitation/reminder for annual fund; said he would let me know if he connects with a special focus in Honors, & I invited him to simply send donations directly to Honors if he wished

- Found it a bit hard to connect with him conversationally; he was animated in catching me up on his career and recounting memories and stories of the campus but not all that receptive when I talked a bit about current Honors achievements

- Probably not a likely candidate for a major gift at this time; should be encouraged to continue and increase annual gifts to Honors Discretionary

Connie Comfort—Contact Notes

Visit by Director H & Development Officer Gerald Greed, April 7, 200_, Chicago, met at Palmer House, then lunch at Russian Tea Room nearby.

- President of Chicago Alumni Chapter, holds regular events

- Owns own business (PR Solutions, Inc.) but also teaches part-time at Chicago State and loves teaching; never wanted to teach in public schools, but college age is good

- Was founding president of our public relations student association and won a competition for a PR campaign

- Husband also an alum, but not honors; has two girls 10 & 8
- Does Relay for Life, kayaks, very active with family outings
- Told her about two of our star PR students, new Honors Center (offered a tour next time she's in town)
- Left Honors packet, note cards, squeezy brains for her girls
- Suggested that she think about a scholarship for an Honors PR student, and she said, "That would be my passion."

APPENDIX D:
ANNOTATED BIBLIOGRAPHY

Brittingham, Barbara E., and Thomas R. Pezzullo. *The Campus Green: Fund Raising in Higher Education.* ASHE-ERIC Higher Education Research Report No. 1. Washington, DC: School of Education and Human Development, The George Washington University, 1990.

This meta-analysis of research on college fundraising notes trends (e.g., in donor behavior) that have continued since its publication. This is not a how-to manual, but its chapters on donor motivation and on ethical issues are especially fruitful reading.

Carnicom, Scott, and Philip M. Mathis. "Building an Honors Development Board." *Honors in Practice* 5 (2009): 41–46.

This account of the establishment of the Board of Visitors at the University Honors College at Middle Tennessee State University discusses the issues surrounding the formation of such a board, including its role in fundraising, and offers a useful model.

Golden, Susan. *Secrets of Successful Grantsmanship: A Guerilla Guide to Raising Money.* San Francisco: Jossey-Bass, 1997.

This is an excellent, practical, comprehensive guide to every stage in the process of seeking grant support. Its distinctive strength is an insistence that success depends on cultivating personal relationships with the funding sources.

Hall, Margarete Rooney. *The Dean's Role in Fund Raising.* Baltimore and London: The Johns Hopkins UP, 1993.

This is a useful book, especially the first three chapters, despite being focused on deans of degree-granting colleges and on issues of structure and management. Written by an academic development officer, it came in the first stages of the trend toward decentralization of fundraising and draws heavily on an empirical study of attitudes and practices among deans and development officers.

Lord, James Gregory. *The Raising of Money: Thirty-Five Essentials Every Trustee Should Know.* Cleveland, OH: Third Sector P, 1983.

Lord is good at setting forth basic principles here and in several other books (*Building Your Case, Communicating with Donors, Philanthropy and Marketing*), principles that have stood the test of time.

Pray, Francis C., ed. *Handbook for Educational Fund Raising: A Guide to Successful Principles and Practices for Colleges, Universities, and Schools.* San Francisco: Jossey-Bass, 1981.

This large collection of essays covers the title topic comprehensively but is addressed mainly to professional development officers and is now a bit outdated. If the institutional library or development office has a copy, it is still worth looking at for its range and its specific examples.

Rhodes, Frank H. T., ed. *Successful Fund Raising for Higher Education.* Phoenix, AZ: American Council on Education and Oryx P, Series on Higher Education, 1997.

This anthology offers macrocosmic overviews of fundraising structures, methods, and successes by institutional type, each chapter focusing on a representative institution (e.g., two-year, women's, black, liberal arts, research, both public and private).

Savage, Tracy G., Irene M. Bunin, Jeanne McKown, Marcia Novak, Tammy L. Ruda, and Sherry Noden. *Donor Relations: The Essential Guide to Stewardship Policies, Procedures, and Protocol.* Washington: Council for the Advancement and Support of Education, 1999.

This is just one of many excellent CASE guides to specific aspects of fundraising. Although it is addressed to professional development officers, its sound principles and its large collection of sample documents make it a useful basic reference. Chapter 5 on organizing recognition societies is especially thorough.

Worth, M. J., ed. *Educational Fund Raising: Principles and Practice.* American Council on Education. Phoenix: Oryx P, 1993.

Designed to update Pray's anthology, this collection by 36 authors covers fundraising comprehensively on the institutional level, though its advice can be extrapolated for an academic unit. Especially useful are Chapters 8–9 on annual giving with their advice on methods of solicitation, Chapters 10–12 on major gifts with tips on record-keeping and solicitation, Chapter 16 on corporate support, Chapter 19 on raising funds from parents, and Chapters 26–27 on the role of public relations and alumni relations in fundraising.

Websites

http://foundationcenter.org

This is the most important and comprehensive information resource about foundation grants, some information free, some by subscription, some available at regional and local reference centers; it is described further in Chapter 1.

http://www.afpnet.org

The Association of Fundraising Professionals claims to be the world's largest such organization and offers a magazine (*Advancing Philanthropy*), a bookstore, and many other resources, including workshops, aimed broadly at professional non-profit development officers, in contrast to the narrower educational focus of CASE. Local chapters abound and may offer a workshop nearby.

http://www.case.org

The Council for Advancement and Support of Education is the best overall resource for fundraisers in higher education, offering a bookstore, a magazine (*Currents*), workshops, and other resources useful both for the professional development officer and the academic.

http://www.goettler.com

An example of a fundraising consultant, Goettler Associates, Inc., Fund-Raising Counsel offers besides its consultancy several free resources, including an online quarterly newsletter (*Fund Raising Matters*). Such consultants are usually members of the Giving Institute (formerly the American Association of Fund-Raising Counsel)—see http://www.givinginstitute.org.

http://www.philanthropy.iupui.edu

This site for the Indiana University Center on Philanthropy, a major philanthropic studies degree-granting institution, includes an extremely useful annotated bibliography under the link to "The Fund Raising School."

NCHC PUBLICATION ORDER FORM

Purchases may be made by calling (402) 472-9150, emailing nchc@unlserve.unl.edu, or mailing a check or money order payable to: NCHC • University of Nebraska-Lincoln 1100 Neihardt Residence Center • 540 N. 16th Street • Lincoln, NE 68588-0627.

FEIN 52–1188042

	Member	Non-Member	No. of Copies	Amount This Item
Monographs:				
Assessing and Evaluating Honors Programs and Honors Colleges: A Practical Handbook	$25.00	$45.00		
Beginning in Honors: A Handbook (4th Ed.)	$25.00	$45.00		
Fundrai$ing for Honor$: A Handbook	$25.00	$45.00		
A Handbook for Honors Administrators	$25.00	$45.00		
A Handbook for Honors Programs at Two-Year Colleges	$25.00	$45.00		
The Honors College Phenomenon	$25.00	$45.00		
Honors Composition: Historical Perspectives and Contemporary Practices	$25.00	$45.00		
Honors Programs at Smaller Colleges (2nd Ed.)	$25.00	$45.00		
Inspiring Exemplary Teaching and Learning: Perspectives on Teaching Academically Talented College Students	$25.00	$45.00		
Place as Text: Approaches to Active Learning	$25.00	$45.00		
Shatter the Glassy Stare: Implementing Experiential Learning in Higher Education	$25.00	$45.00		
Teaching and Learning in Honors	$25.00	$45.00		
Journals & Other Publications:				
Journal of the National Collegiate Honors Council (JNCHC) *Specify Vol/Issue ___/___*	$25.00	$45.00		
Honors in Practice (HIP) *Specify Vol ___*	$25.00	$45.00		
Peterson's Smart Choices (The official NCHC guide to Honors Programs & Colleges)	$20.00	$29.95		

Total Copies Ordered and Total Amount Paid: _____ $ _____

Apply a 20% discount if 10+ copies are purchased.

Name _____

Institution _____

Address _____

City, State, Zip _____

Phone _____ Fax _____ Email _____

NATIONAL COLLEGIATE HONORS COUNCIL
MONOGRAPHS & JOURNALS

Assessing and Evaluating Honors Programs and Honors Colleges: A Practical Handbook by Rosalie Otero and Robert Spurrier (2005, 98pp). This monograph includes an overview of assessment and evaluation practices and strategies. It explores the process for conducting self-studies and discusses the differences between using consultants and external reviewers. It provides a guide to conducting external reviews along with information about how to become an NCHC-Recommended Site Visitor. A dozen appendices provide examples of "best practices."

Beginning in Honors: A Handbook by Samuel Schuman (Fourth Edition, 2006, 80pp). Advice on starting a new honors program. Covers budgets, recruiting students and faculty, physical plant, administrative concerns, curriculum design, and descriptions of some model programs.

Fundrai$ing for Honor$: A Handbook by Larry R. Andrews (2009, 160pp). Offers information and advice on raising money for honors, beginning with easy first steps and progressing to more sophisticated and ambitious fundraising activities.

A Handbook for Honors Administrators by Ada Long (1995, 117pp). Everything an honors administrator needs to know, including a description of some models of honors administration.

A Handbook for Honors Programs at Two-Year Colleges by Theresa James (2006, 136pp). A useful handbook for two-year schools contemplating beginning or redesigning their honors program and for four-year schools doing likewise or wanting to increase awareness about two-year programs and articulation agreements. Contains extensive appendices about honors contracts and a comprehensive bibliography on honors education.

The Honors College Phenomenon edited by Peter C. Sederberg (2008, 172pp). This monograph examines the growth of honors colleges since 1990: historical and descriptive characterizations of the trend, alternative models that include determining whether becoming a college is appropriate, and stories of creation and recreation. Leaders whose institutions are contemplating or taking this step as well as those directing established colleges should find these essays valuable.

Honors Composition: Historical Perspectives and Contemporary Practices by Annmarie Guzy (2003, 182pp). Parallel historical developments in honors and composition studies; contemporary honors writing projects ranging from admission essays to theses as reported by over 300 NCHC members.

Honors Programs at Smaller Colleges by Samuel Schuman (Second Edition, 1999, 53pp). How to implement an honors program, with particular emphasis on colleges with fewer than 3000 students.

Inspiring Exemplary Teaching and Learning: Perspectives on Teaching Academically Talented College Students edited by Larry Clark and John Zubizarreta (2008, 216pp). This rich collection of essays offers valuable insights into innovative teaching and significant learning in the context of academically challenging classrooms and programs. The volume provides theoretical, descriptive, and practical resources, including models of effective instructional practices, examples of successful courses designed for enhanced learning, and a list of online links to teaching and learning centers and educational databases worldwide.

Place as Text: Approaches to Active Learning edited by Bernice Braid and Ada Long (2000, 104pp). Information and practical advice on the experiential pedagogies developed within NCHC during the past 25 years, using Honors Semesters and City as Text™ as models, along with suggestions for how to adapt these models to a variety of educational contexts.

Shatter the Glassy Stare: Implementing Experiential Learning in Higher Education edited by Peter A. Machonis (2008, 160pp). A companion piece to *Place as Text*, focusing on recent, innovative applications of City as Text™ teaching strategies. Chapters on campus as text, local neighborhoods, study abroad, science courses, writing exercises, and philosophical considerations, with practical materials for instituting this pedagogy.

Teaching and Learning in Honors edited by Cheryl L. Fuiks and Larry Clark (2000, 128pp). Presents a variety of perspectives on teaching and learning useful to anyone developing new or renovating established honors curricula.

Journal of the National Collegiate Honors Council (JNCHC) is a semi-annual periodical featuring scholarly articles on honors education. Articles may include analyses of trends in teaching methodology, articles on interdisciplinary efforts, discussions of problems common to honors programs, items on the national higher education agenda, and presentations of emergent issues relevant to honors education.

Honors in Practice (HIP) is an annual journal that accommodates the need and desire for articles about nuts-and-bolts practices by featuring practical and descriptive essays on topics such as successful honors courses, suggestions for out-of-class experiences, administrative issues, and other topics of interest to honors administrators, faculty, and students.